Why investors misprice the market and central banks are flirting with disaster

November 21, 2019

By: William P. DeCotiis

Printed in the United States of America.

First Edition: November 2019.

ISBN: 978-0-9962738-7-9

Contents

Introduction 5

The Formula 6

Why is the Formula superior to traditional measurements of price and value? 7

How does the Formula work? 8

Selection of the Risk-Free Rate 10

The Components of the Formula 11

Proportional Relationships 14

Superiority of the Formula 20

Historical Performance 26

Statistical Considerations 34

Log Values and Scaling 35

Mathematical Operation of the Formula 36

Forecasting 37

Assumptions 42

General Applicability Across Industries 44

Pitfalls and Criticism 48

A Speculative View Drawn from the Data 49

Conclusion 50

Appendix A 51

- Part I (Risk-Adjusted CAPE) 51
- Part II (Apple PE Risk-Adjusted) 54

Appendix B 58

- Part A (Wilshire 5000 Datasets) 58
- Part B (S&P Datasets) 63
- Part C (Housing Datasets) 67
- Part D (Cyclical PE Datasets) 69
- Part E (Apple Stock PE Dataset) 74

Introduction

The U.S. equity markets are not over-valued at current levels. However, as little as a 200-basis point increase in the ten-year treasury note rate would cause historic overvaluation in U.S. equity markets. In recent years market indexes have pushed prices to all-time highs. Price to value ratios during this period have similarly reached all time historic highs. This has led many to believe that U.S. equities are over-extended or priced to excess. However, after adjusting for a historically low risk-free rate, it becomes clear that markets are not overvalued at current levels. However, even a mild move in the risk-free rate (assumed in this paper to be the U.S. ten-year treasury note rate) would cause historic over-valuation not seen since the Great Depression or Dot-com bubble.

The Formula

To provide a historic ratio of comparison the following formula is employed.

$R_v = (P \times R_f) / V$

where

R_v is the value of the historical ratio returned by the function

P is the price of the asset, sector, market or index

R_f is the risk-free rate of return (or standard rate in a sector or market)

V is a corresponding value metric of the corresponding asset, sector, market or index

The formula $R_v = (P \times R_f) / V$ (hereinafter the "Formula") provides a relative measure of the expense of any asset, market or economy provided a historical dataset as a comparative reference. In the context of the U.S. equity market inserting values of a total price index for price, the U.S. ten-year treasury note rate for the risk-free rate and gross domestic product for value provides a relative measure of the expense (or lack of expense) of the U.S. equity market. This measure of expense is superior to traditional measures of price to value because it incorporates the risk-free rate and as such market conditions regarding inflation, extension of credit and monetary policy.

Current ratio values compared to historic values calculated using the S&P index, nominal GDP and the quoted ten-year treasury note rate indicate that the price of the S&P can be sustained for time to come. However, (assuming GDP remains relatively constant) any meaningful increase in the ten-year treasury note rate beyond 200 basis points would result in market expense last seen during the Great Depression and Dot-com bubble (with the probable effect being a severe deleveraging and decline in market prices).

Why is the Formula superior to traditional measurements of price and value?

Traditional measurements of the relative expense of global financial markets are falsely reading extremely high triggering concern among investors. The reason these measurements are providing a false positive presently is that they do not account for a historically low risk-free rate, low cost of borrowing and coordinated loose monetary policy being promulgated by central banks around the world.

The U.S. ten-year treasury note rate provides a fair barometer of inflation/deflation expectations and the relative cost of borrowing in the U.S. over a ten-year leading time horizon. For this reason and because of the perceived safety/stability in the U.S. system of government, creditworthiness of the U.S. economy and faith of the international community (and its own citizens) in the U.S. rule of law, the ten-year treasury note rate can be used as the rate of return one can receive risk-free over a ten-year period (or characterized another way, over one business cycle). As such, the rate of return of the ten-year treasury note provides a base level of return that investors expect in making risk-allocations.[1]

Most current models for assessing relative expense in equity markets ignore this generally accepted financial fact and thereby generally ignore the Capital Asset Pricing Model. As such, these popular indicators[2] provide a critical blind spot for investors in that while they provide an accurate depiction of expense of price relative to value (whether in the form of earnings or GDP), these metrics fail to account for the role of the risk-free rate plays in contributing to the spread between price and value. That is to say, these metrics fail to account for the spread between price and value which does not result simply from irrational markets or mispricing, but rather are more accurately attributed to the availability of money, access to credit and a rational assessment of risk-adjusted return when accounting for the value of the risk-free rate of return.

The valuation analysis described below eliminates this blind spot by taking the product of a market's price and the yield of a selected rate (in this case the ten-year treasury note rate as a barometer of the risk-free rate), providing a "risk-adjusted" price metric. This "risk-adjusted" price metric is then divided by a value metric (whether earnings (inflation or cyclically adjusted or otherwise) or GDP (or a similar production metric)) to provide a ratio of the relative risk-adjusted price to the relative production of the market being analyzed. The resulting ratio provides normalized historical data of the relative expense of the analyzed market accounting for the effect of risk-free rate on the price of capital assets.

---

[1] This is the fundamental underpinning of the Capital Asset Pricing Model.

[2] Popular indicators of this nature include Market Capitalization to GDP or Stock Index to GDP and Price to Earnings ratios (whether cyclically adjusted or otherwise).

How does the Formula work?

In its simplest form the Formula identifies three components that are responsible for determining expected returns of any asset on a risk-adjusted basis: 1) price 2) value and 3) the risk of receipt of the expected value. That is to say, the price paid divided by the production value realized adjusted against the risk-free rate of return.

In the context of assets and markets, the price of an asset or market can increase or decrease in accordance with demand. When price increases without a corresponding increase in underlying production value, the price of the market/asset becomes more "expensive". That is to say, the cost of acquiring the production value of the asset or market increases and therefore returns from that production decrease. When price decreases without a corresponding decrease in underlying production value, the price of the market/asset becomes "cheaper". That is to say, the cost of acquiring the production value of the asset or market decreases and therefore returns from that production increase. As can be intuited, purchasing assets when they are priced "cheaply" will result in higher returns than purchasing assets when they are priced "expensively" provided there is no change in underlying productive value.

In the context of assets and markets, the value of an asset or market is determined by the production of that asset or market. This can be measured in a number of ways, but in the context of markets this most often takes the form of "earnings" or in the context of the U.S. economy, gross domestic product. If an asset's or market's ability to produce increases, the value of the asset or market increases. If an asset's or market's ability to produce decreases, the value of the asset or market decreases. If an asset's or market's value increases without a corresponding change in price, the cost of acquiring the productive value of the asset or market decreases and the asset/market becomes "cheaper". If an asset's or market's value decreases without a corresponding change in price, the cost of acquiring the productive value of the asset or market increases and the asset/market becomes more "expensive". As can be intuited, purchasing assets when they are priced "cheaply" will result in higher returns than purchasing assets when they are priced "expensively".

For all assets and markets, there is a risk that the production value of the purchased asset or market will not materialize after it is acquired. This risk requires compensation in the form of additional return or a "risk-premium". Said another way, to a rational investor production that is consistent and guaranteed to materialize is more attractive than production that is inconsistent (i.e. volatile) or speculative (i.e. unlikely to materialize). To induce rational investors to risk capital to acquire the production of an asset which is volatile or potentially at risk of not materializing (a so-called "risk asset"), additional return must be offered to compensate against the risk of loss of that production (in either the form of additional future production or a lower purchase price).

Because of the risk of loss of production value inherent in all productive assets, all assets (and all markets comprised of productive assets) are priced relative to the return an investor can receive without any risk of loss (termed the "risk-free return" under the Capital Asset Pricing Model).[3] Under the Capital Asset Pricing Model, all assets are priced in accordance with a premium of return beyond the return which could be achieved "risk-free" (in proportion to the risk of loss of the risk asset).[4] As can be

[3] https://www.investopedia.com/articles/06/capm.asp

[4] https://www.investopedia.com/articles/06/capm.asp

intuited, an asset or market will be unattractive to rational investors if the return which can be achieved "risk-free" is greater than or equal to the return which can be achieved from "risk assets" and the demand for "risk-assets" will decrease. Conversely, an asset or market will be attractive to rational investors if the return which can be achieved "risk-free" is less than the return which can be achieved from "risk assets" and the demand for "risk assets" will increase. Said simply, rational investors will seek assets or markets with the greatest possible return for the least amount of risk all things being equal.[5] As a result, if the risk-free rate increases, the relative price of risk-assets must correspondingly decrease to account for the return per unit of risk lost by risk-assets as the risk-free rate increases. Conversely, if the risk-free rate decreases, the relative price of risk-assets must correspondingly increase to account for the return per unit of risk gained by risk-assets as the risk-free rate decreases.

When price, value and the risk-free rate are considered together one can see that if price rises, production drops, or the risk-free rate increases an asset becomes more expensive if the other components are held constant. Conversely, if price drops, production rises or the risk-free rate decreases an asset becomes cheaper if the other components are held constant. As can be intuited, each of these components is dynamic and tend to change while the other components are changing as well. By analyzing these components in the Formula described, the proportion by which these components move can be measured overtime. These measurements can be effectively utilized to identify relative "cheapness" and "expensiveness" in an asset or market on a risk-adjusted basis.

Additionally, because in most economies lending rates are based on the risk-free rate, in addition to its role in risk-allocations, the risk-free rate tends to serve as a fair approximation for the availability of credit. That is to say, the cost of borrowing is lower when the risk-free rate is low, because interest rates of loans are pegged to the risk-free rate. As a result, when the risk-free rate is low, borrowers tend to borrow more because there is an incentive to borrow and invest in risk-assets to acquire the spread between the cost of borrowing and the expected return of risk-assets.

Similarly, because the risk-free rate tends to be the lending rate of a stable national government and the lending rate of a stable national government tends to be a tool used by central bankers and policy makers to stabilize national currency (by raising rates when inflation is present and decreasing rates when deflation is present to maintain a neutral rate where currency supply and credit extension is stable), inclusion of the risk-free rate in the Formula also approximates relative monetary supply.[6]

As a result, the supply of credit, the monetary supply and risk-adjusted asset pricing become incorporated into the Formula by way of inclusion of the "risk-free" rate.

---

[5] There also tends to be a general bias in modern markets for a baseline of return somewhere between 5-10% annualized which drives decision making.

[6] It should be noted however that for data sets extending multiple decades it may be necessary to adjust for inflation in both the price data and the value data to prevent distortions in Formula output.

Selection of the Risk-Free Rate

For purposes of the analysis here, the yield on the ten-year U.S. treasury note will be the stated "risk-free rate". However, it is important to note that any "risk-free rate" which is an accurate reflection of the risk-free rate of the relevant economy can be used provided it provides a fair barometer of inflation/deflation expectations, the relative cost of borrowing, and is perceived as safe and stable (i.e. the creditworthiness of the economy and the faith of the national/international community in the rule of law). In the United States treasury bills/notes are generally believed to have the full faith and credit of the U.S. government (and therethrough the U.S. taxpayer). The U.S. economy is viewed as highly creditworthy and productive and the rule of law in the U.S. is considered by its citizens and the international community to be stable, functional and just.

In selecting a risk-free rate, the maturity of the rate is also highly relevant. Generally speaking, shorter duration maturities are viewed as less risky since capital is at risk for a short period and the return must be generated within that short period (making it less likely either principal or expected return will be lost). As such, one would expect to use the shortest maturity duration available as the risk-free rate (one could certainly do so). However, because of certain characteristics of short-term rates in the U.S., the analysis conducted herein uses the ten-year treasury note rate. As an initial matter, in the U.S. short-term rates are significantly influenced by the central bank (the Federal Reserve Board) and as a result, tend to not fully reflect general market views on inflation/deflation or future borrowing costs because of the weight in which the federal reserve exercises control over such rate. Additionally, because the typical business cycle in the U.S. tends to last approximately ten years, the ten-year treasury note rate provides a fair assessment of the forward-looking risk-free expectations of the marketplace (i.e. the ten-year forecast of the marketplace). Said another way, the ten-year treasury note provides the base level of return that investors expect to receive in making risk-allocations over the course of a business cycle.

Similarly, one could effectively use a longer-term rate (such as the thirty-year treasury note rate for instance). However, as beforementioned, this rate tends to be less nimble and less focused on business cycles due to the long-duration of the rate. Because a business cycle tends to represent the trading/investing time horizon of most investors/traders, the ten-year treasury note rate will be used for purposes of this analysis.

The Components of the Formula

Price

The first component of the Formula is price data. Price data can be for an individual asset or index. For purposes of this analysis the Wilshire 5000 will be used as a measure of total market capitalization of the U.S. equity market for price (such data sourced from the Federal Reserve Bank of St. Louis).

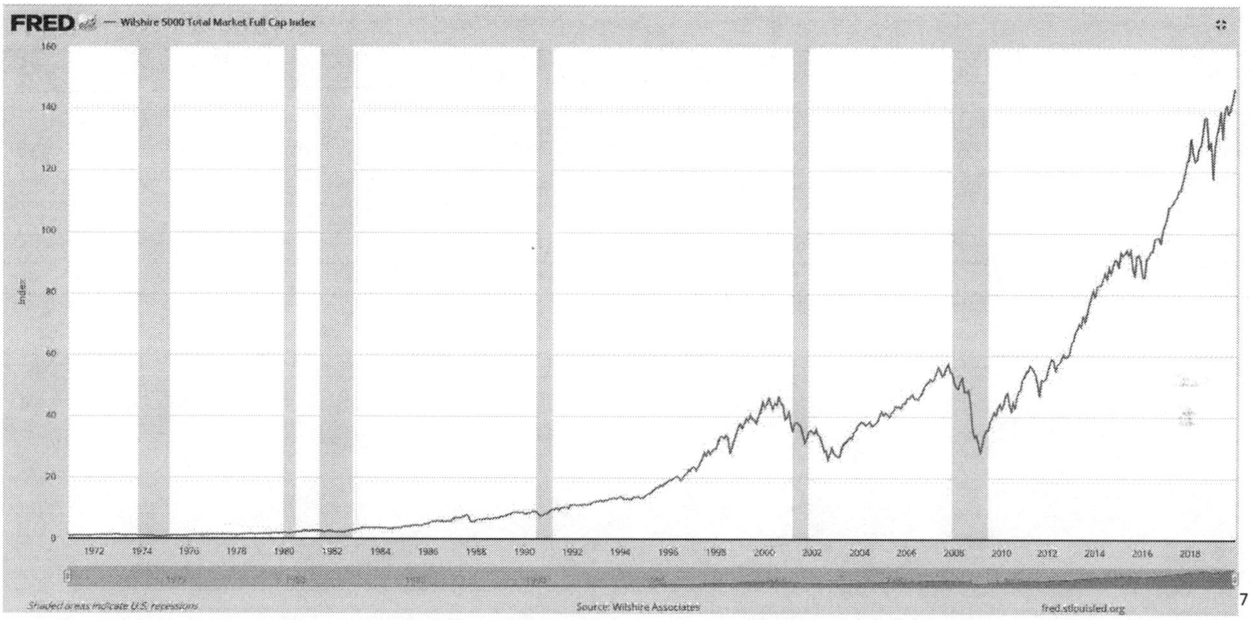

[7]

As can be seen, just looking at price does not provide sufficient data to determine if a market is over- or under-valued. Investors often mistakenly believe that a market is too expensive because it is at an all-time high or believe it is inexpensive because it is at a historical low. While coincidentally this may be periodically true, price itself and its relative high or low does not provide meaningful information in determining whether a market is over- or under-valued. However, analyzing price relative to the other components of the Formula provides meaningful output.

[7] Wilshire Associates, Wilshire 5000 Total Market Full Cap Index [WILL5000INDFC], retrieved from FRED, Federal Reserve Bank of St. Louis; https://fred.stlouisfed.org/series/WILL5000INDFC, November 21, 2019.

The second component of the Formula is value data. This can be the productive value of an individual asset, a market, or an economy corresponding with the price data sourced. For purposes of this analysis U.S. nominal GDP sourced from the Federal Reserve Bank of St. Louis is used as a measure of the productive value of the U.S. economy since U.S. nominal GDP as a measure of value corresponds with the price data of total U.S. market capitalization.

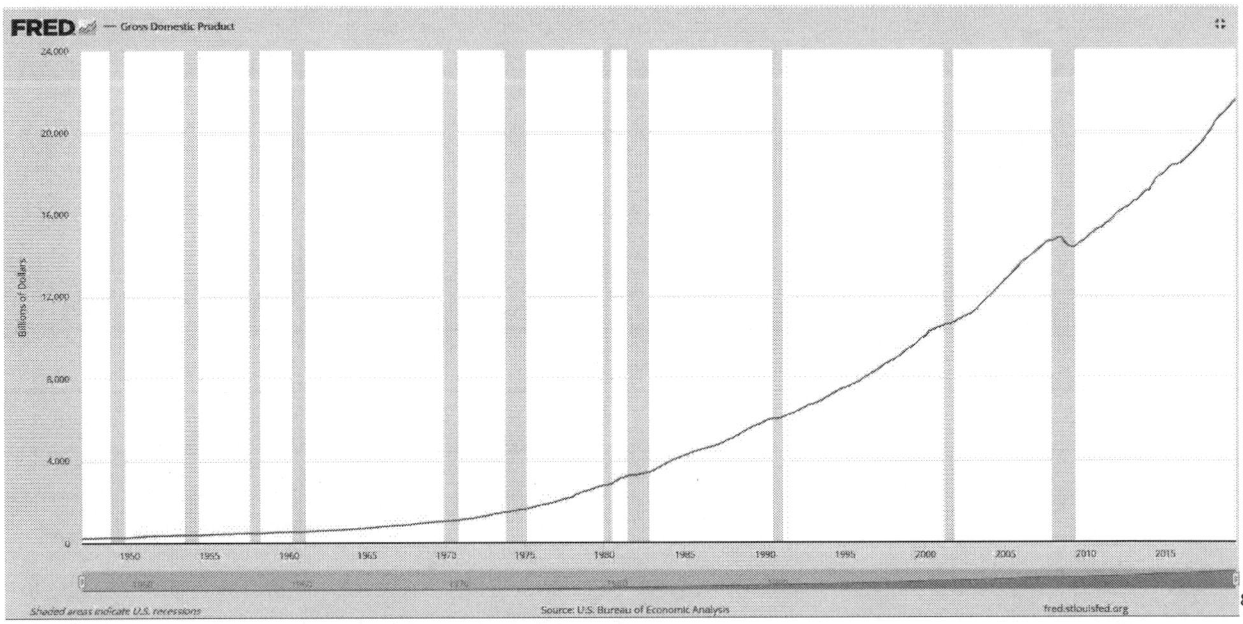

[8]

Value data is accurate in determining the overall increase or decrease in production that an asset, market or economy is experiencing. However, value alone is not an indication of return, since a price must be paid to acquire a productive asset. As such, return can only be determined by considering value in the context of the price required to acquire the productive asset.

[8] U.S. Bureau of Economic Analysis, Gross Domestic Product [GDP], retrieved from FRED, Federal Reserve Bank of St. Louis; https://fred.stlouisfed.org/series/GDP, November 20, 2019.

The risk-free rate fluctuates with time as a result of supply and demand forces. The primary forces which contribute to fluctuations in supply and demand of the risk-free asset tend to be the stability of the government, expectations of inflation/deflation and prevailing views on the expansion or restriction of credit (and to a lesser extent general speculative views about future market returns and the perceived safety of risk assets). Generally speaking, in the U.S., the economy and government are perceived as safe and stable so inflation/deflation expectations as well as governmental attitudes toward credit tend to be the primary factors affecting moves in the ten-year treasury note rate (along with short-term speculative views about perceived risk in risk-assets).

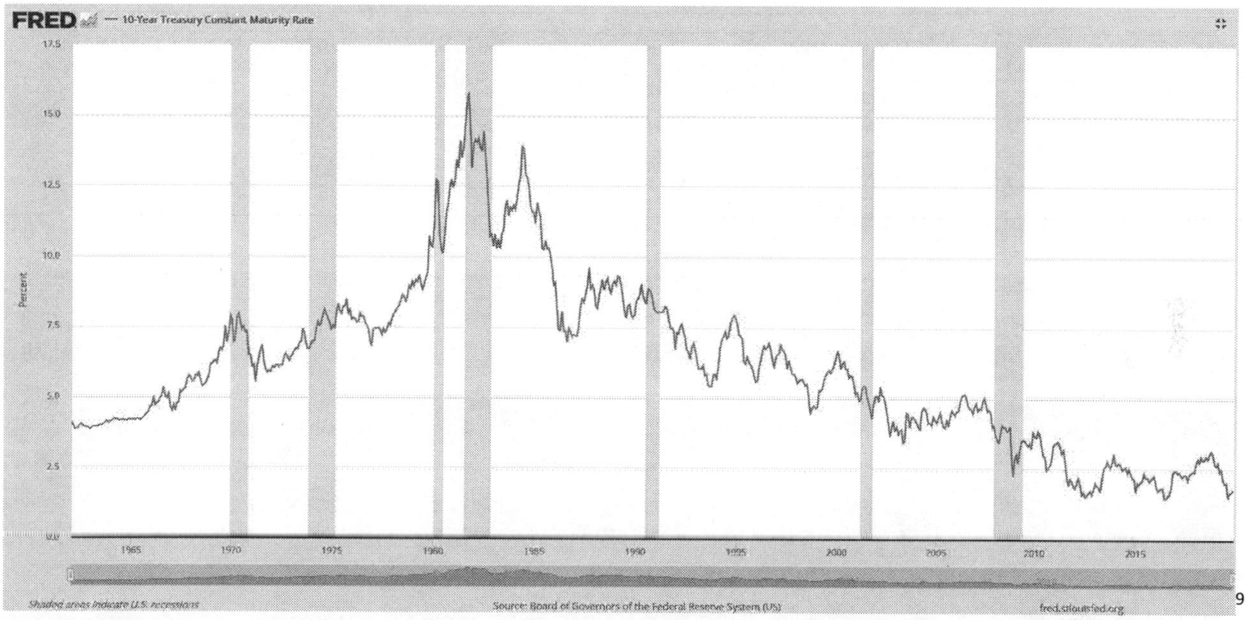

[9]

From the chart above, one can clearly see that after rising from the 1960s until the 1980s (tracking inflation among other things) from the 1980s onward the ten-year treasury note rate has consistently declined with time as deflation has taken hold and the U.S. government has pursued a general policy toward credit expansion. Deflation and credit expansion generally contribute to increases in the price of risk assets, while inflation and credit contraction generally contribute to decreases in the price of risk assets.

[9] Board of Governors of the Federal Reserve System (US), 10-Year Treasury Constant Maturity Rate [DGS10], retrieved from FRED, Federal Reserve Bank of St. Louis; https://fred.stlouisfed.org/series/DGS10, November 21, 2019.

Proportional Relationships

Price to Value Ratio

Price and value are inherently linked by nature of the fact all assets are rationally priced by taking the productive value of an asset over a selected time frame and discounting that value back to the present day (plus a premium based on demand/attractiveness of such productivity). Overtime price tends to reflect increases or decreases in underlying value. Further price tends to revert to value in the long run despite short-term periods of episodic swings of under- and over-extensions in price.

One can measure the relationship between price and value through use of a ratio of price to value. Dividing price by value and expression as a ratio is useful because it identifies the per unit price for each unit of value.

Once expressed as a ratio, the relative expense of an asset becomes evident by nature of the per unit price for value relationship over a given time horizon.

To generate this ratio, one takes price data and divides it by the value data of the corresponding time period. For purposes of this analysis, the Wilshire 5000 is divided by U.S. nominal GDP in quarterly intervals over the time period identified on the chart.

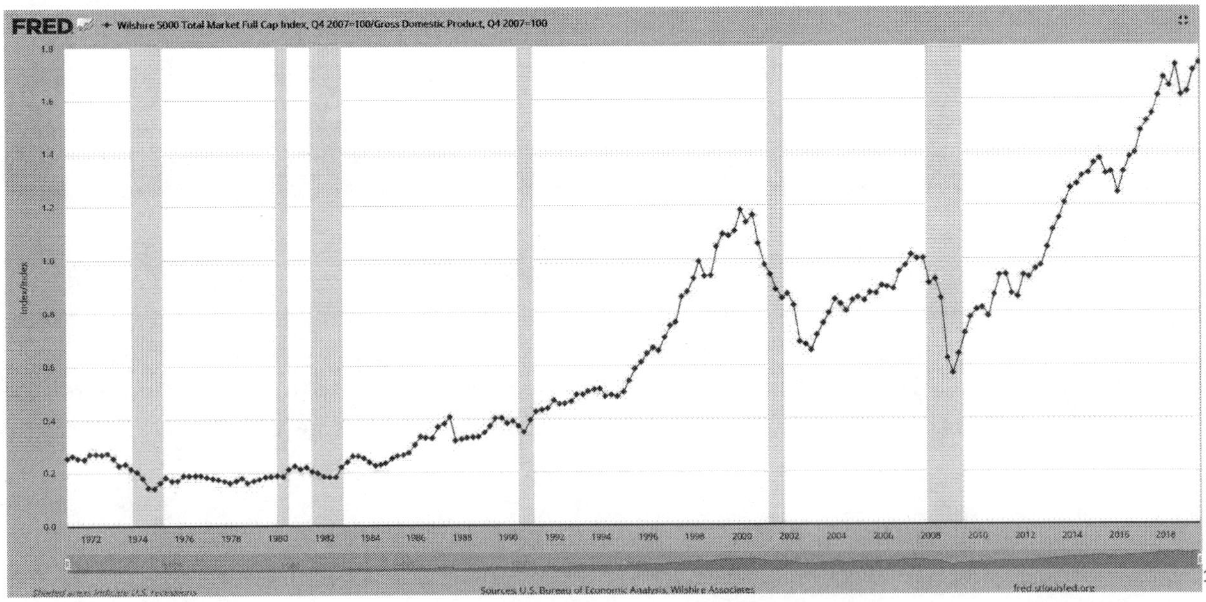

[10]

[10] Wilshire Associates, Wilshire 5000 Total Market Full Cap Index [WILL5000INDFC], retrieved from FRED, Federal Reserve Bank of St. Louis; https://fred.stlouisfed.org/series/WILL5000INDFC, November 21, 2019. U.S. Bureau of Economic Analysis, Gross Domestic Product [GDP], retrieved from FRED, Federal Reserve Bank of St. Louis; https://fred.stlouisfed.org/series/GDP, November 21, 2019.

This ratio is a highly effective measure of the relative expense of the equity markets (or said another way an effective way of measuring the variance between price and value). However, it has one critical failure. It fails to adjust for risk, credit or inflation/deflation. By way of example, based on the graph above, in the year 2015, it seems quite clear that the market is expensive. Yet for the next 4 years market prices remain elevated. One might surmise that this is because markets are irrational. However, after factoring in the risk-free rate it becomes clear that such expense is rational on a risk-adjusted basis.[11]

[11] Although to be sure the market certainly exhibits episodic irrationality.

The Product of Price and the Risk-Free Rate

As can be seen from the chart below, the relative performance of the market has increased since the 1980s as the ten-year treasury note rate has fallen. This is not entirely due to the decrease in the ten-year treasury note rate (as the value of the market increased during this period as evidenced by the Price/Value discussion above), however, deflationary expectations together with a prevalent policy toward credit expansion in the U.S. is clearly correlated with increasing risk-asset prices.

To evidence the relationship of price and the risk-free rate, one multiplies the price data by the risk-free rate. Doing so, creates a proportional relationship between price and the risk-free rate such that increases in the risk-free rate necessarily increase the measurement of price and decreases in the risk-free rate proportionately decrease price. While not mathematically precise, adjusting the price by the risk-free rate in this way has the effect of normalizing price relative to monetary supply (i.e. the availability of credit, inflation/deflation expectations, and general supply of money). Said another way, when the risk-free rate is high, inflation is likely high, credit is likely less available/more difficult to service and there is, generally speaking, less monetary value available for making purchases. As a result of this relative scarcity in purchasing power, the per unit price of items is "more expensive" than nominally observed and as such more "price" is included in the product. Conversely, when the risk-free rate is low, inflation is likely low, credit is likely more available/easier to service and there is generally speaking more monetary value available for making purchases. As a result of this relative surplus in purchasing power, the per unit price of items is "cheaper" than nominally observed and as such less "price" is included in the product. Thus, multiplying the risk-free rate by nominal price proportionally impacts price in accordance with the relative attractiveness of the risk-assets.

As can be seen from the chart below, when price is considered together with the risk-free rate, movement in the risk-free rate can exacerbate or diminish the impact of movements in market price.

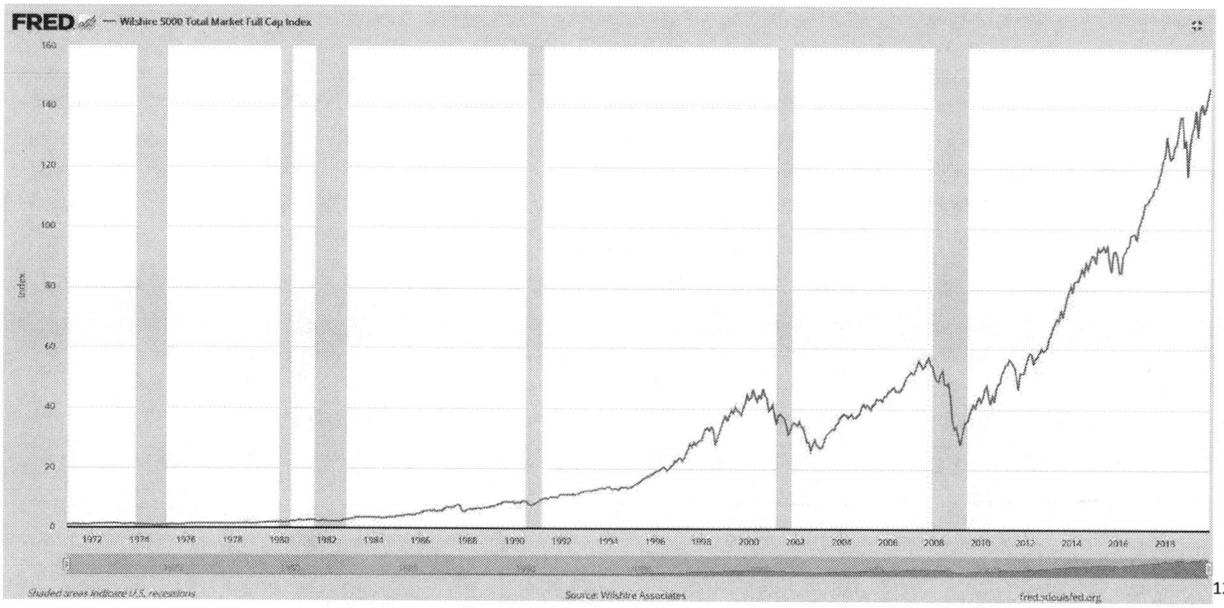

[12]

[12] Wilshire Associates, Wilshire 5000 Total Market Full Cap Index [WILL5000INDFC], retrieved from FRED, Federal Reserve Bank of St. Louis; https://fred.stlouisfed.org/series/WILL5000INDFC, November 21, 2019.

From the proportional relationships described above, it is clear that 1) there is, for any asset, at any given time a unit price for each unit of value acquired which is expressed by the ratio of price to value, and 2) there is a proportional relationship between the risk-free rate and price such that as the risk-free rate increases relative purchasing power decreases and as the risk-free rate decreases purchasing power increases.

Combining these relationships into one formula provides a more holistic view than either relationship alone, since each of the three variables described plays an independent role in the function's determination of the output. Said in economic terms, the Formula measures the unit price of value accounting for the approximate availability of purchasing power.

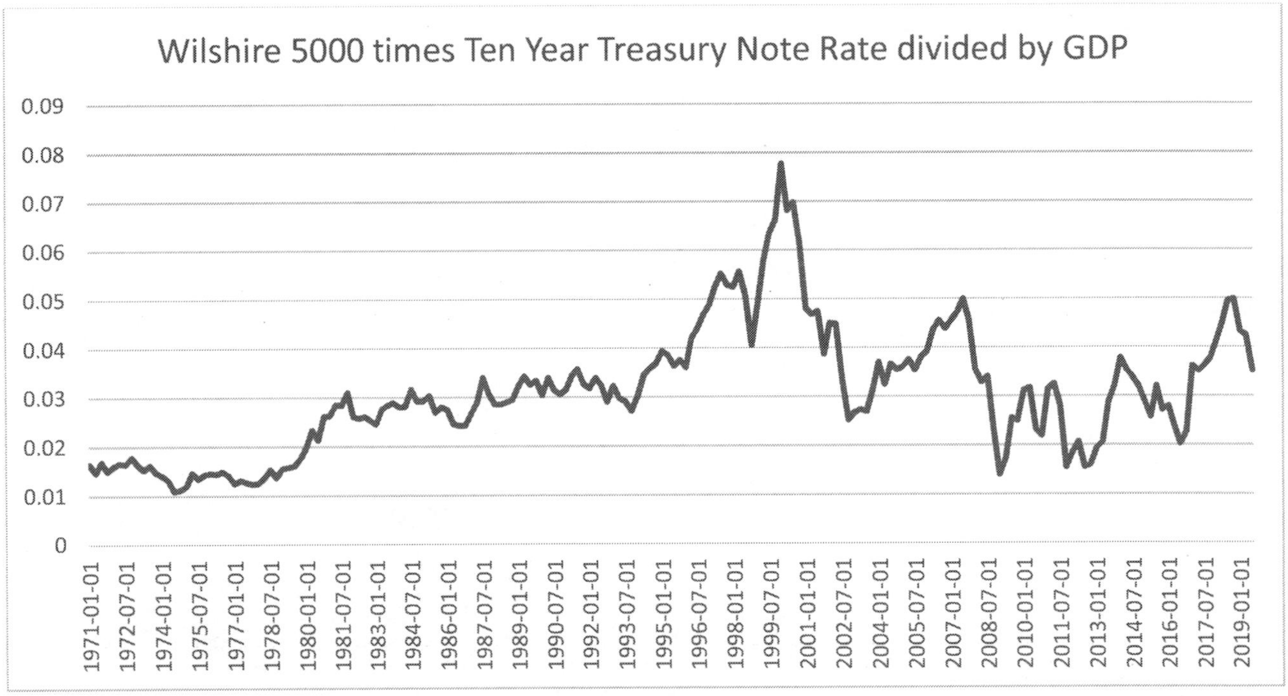

Since 1971 (the year in which the U.S. officially detached the U.S. currency from the gold standard), the historical average ratio of the Formula is 0.03 with a standard deviation of 0.013.[13]

As can be seen from the chart above, the U.S. equity markets were undervalued throughout all of the 1970s and 1980s until late 1990s, since statistically speaking, the U.S. equity markets remained under the historical average until such period. In the first quarter of 2000, the U.S. equity market became historically expensive (more than three standard deviations above the historical mean). After a historic market collapse, by mid-2002, the equity market was priced near the historical average, until again becoming overpriced in the second quarter of 2007 (approximately two standard deviations above the historical mean). Following another collapse, the market became highly underpriced in the first quarter

[13] Two standard deviations are +/-0.025. Three standard deviations are +/-0.38.

of 2009 (approximately one standard deviation below the historical mean) and has remained underpriced until October 2018 (again two standard deviations above the historical mean).

In recent memory it may be easy to recall that October 2018 marked a ~20% sell-off in the U.S. equity markets, which was swiftly met by a series of central bank rate cuts (approximately 200 basis points). Which has brought the relative expensiveness of the current market near the historical mean.

Superiority of the Formula

The Formula compared to an analysis of price alone

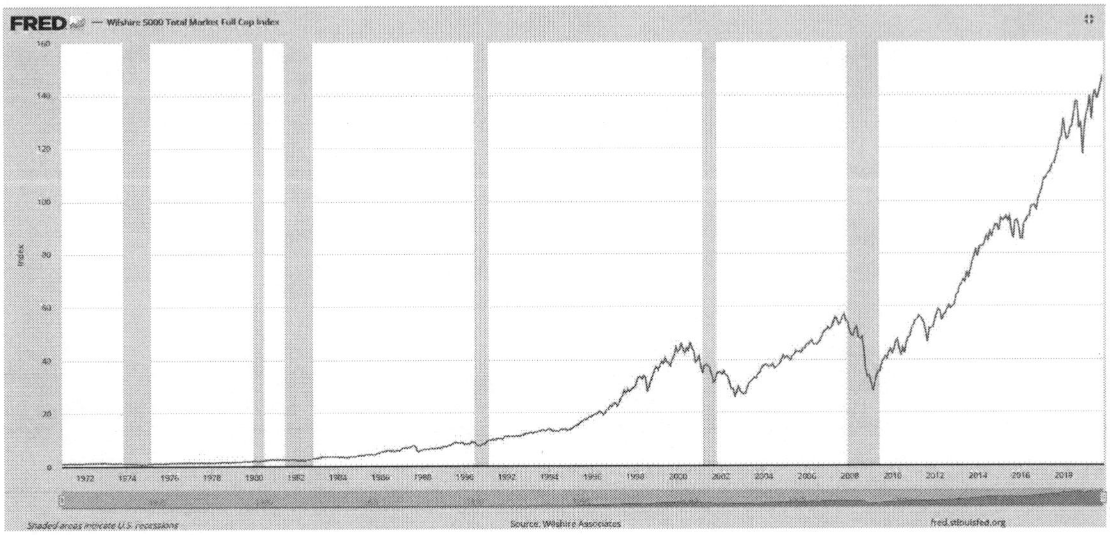

[14]

Given the benefit of hindsight, one can observe that a mere chart of price fails to consider relative expense. In 2000, the market was at a historic high, but it would be difficult in real time to measure just how poor returns over the next ten years would be if one bought during the height of 2000. However, looking at the Formula it is obvious that the market had reached a historic expense which was likely to cause inferior returns over the next 10 years to come.

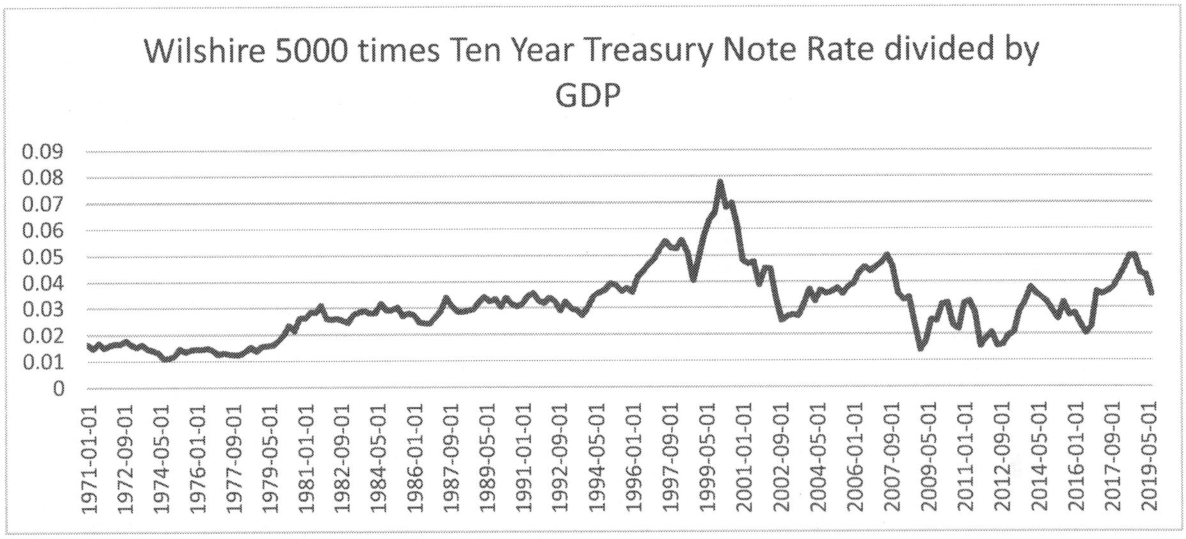

[14] Wilshire Associates, Wilshire 5000 Total Market Full Cap Index [WILL5000INDFC], retrieved from FRED, Federal Reserve Bank of St. Louis; https://fred.stlouisfed.org/series/WILL5000INDFC, November 21, 2019.

In 2007, the price of the market once again appears at a historic high, however the Formula indicates that while expensive, the market was not as expensive as in 2000 (despite being priced similar nominally). Even if one bought in the height of the 2007 financial crisis, one still enjoyed significant returns over the next ten years.

Clearly, price alone cannot be relied upon for making investment or policy decisions.

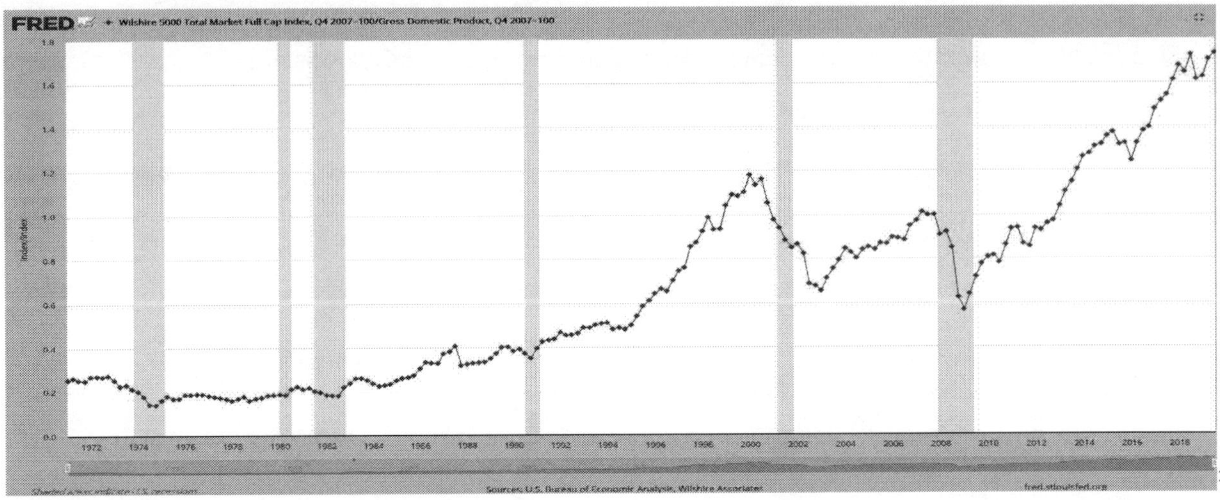

[15]

Given the benefit of hindsight, one can see that measuring price in the context of value provides a superior lens with which to view the relative expense of the market. In early 2000, the ratio of price to value clearly identifies historic expensiveness. After the collapse of this bubble, the ratio indicates relative inexpensiveness, prior to once again reaching historic expensiveness in 2007 (but not as high as 2000). Following another decline in prices, the ratio identifies inexpensiveness before reaching historic expensiveness in 2014 (equivalent to Dot-com era expensiveness). Since 2014, the historic expensiveness of the market has steadily increased reaching a historically unprecedented level (nearly double Dot-com and financial crisis levels of expense).

[15] Wilshire Associates, Wilshire 5000 Total Market Full Cap Index [WILL5000INDFC], retrieved from FRED, Federal Reserve Bank of St. Louis; https://fred.stlouisfed.org/series/WILL5000INDFC, November 21, 2019. U.S. Bureau of Economic Analysis, Gross Domestic Product [GDP], retrieved from FRED, Federal Reserve Bank of St. Louis; https://fred.stlouisfed.org/series/GDP, November 21, 2019.

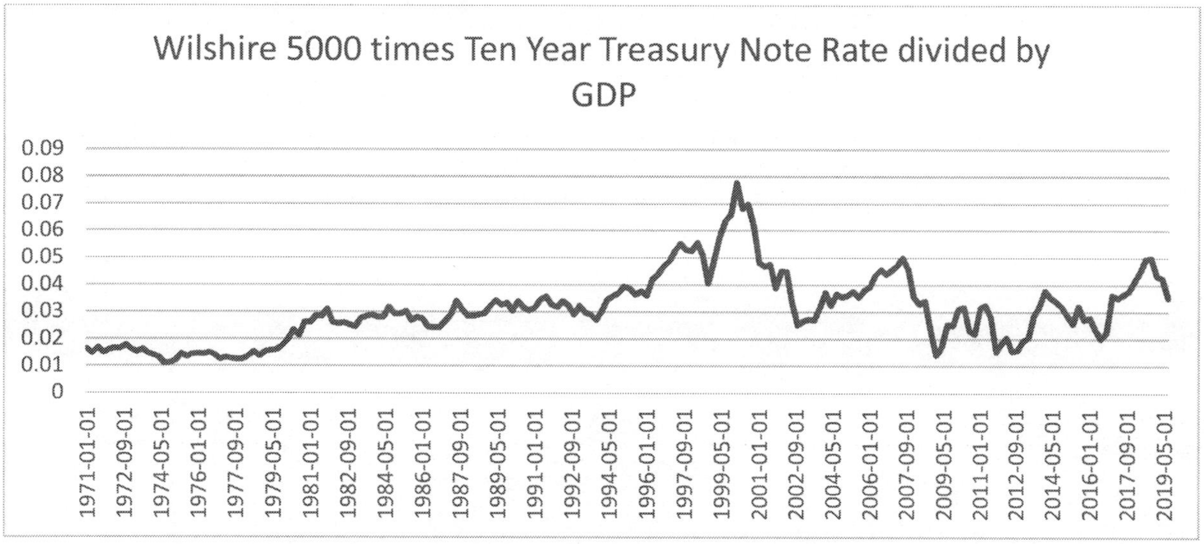

Looking at price to value alone would be a cause of extraordinary concern for a rational investor (perhaps it still should). However, when considered in the context of the risk-free rate, as evidenced by the Formula, it becomes clear that the market did not truly reach a historic level of expense until early 2018, at which point the federal reserve acted promptly to reduce the risk-free rate reducing the relative expensiveness brought on by steadily increasing equity prices (without corresponding increases in gross productive value).

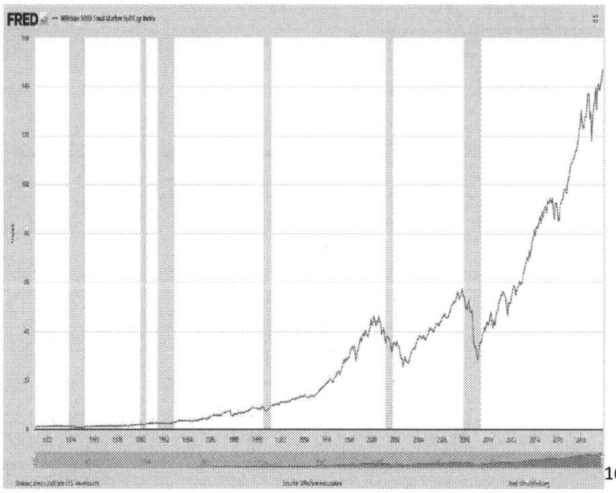

[16]

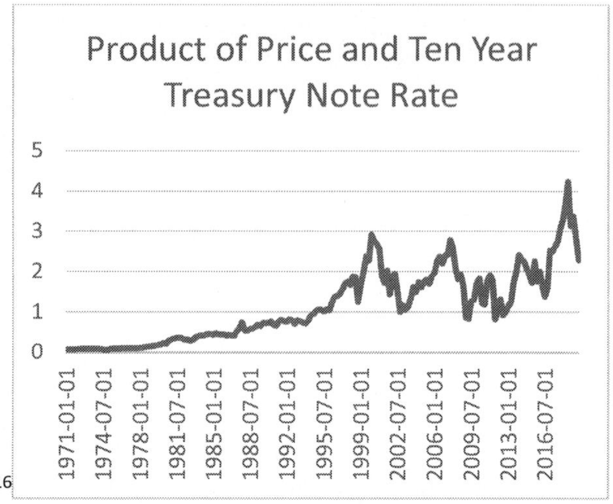

Given the benefit of hindsight, one can see that measuring price in the context of the risk-free rate provides a superior lens with which to view the relative expense of the market than price alone.

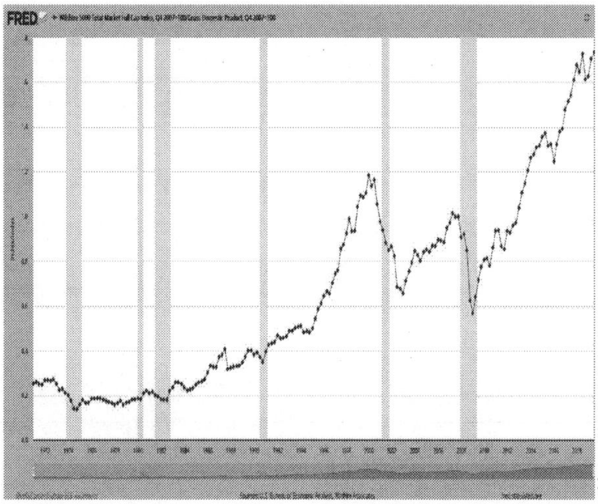

[17]

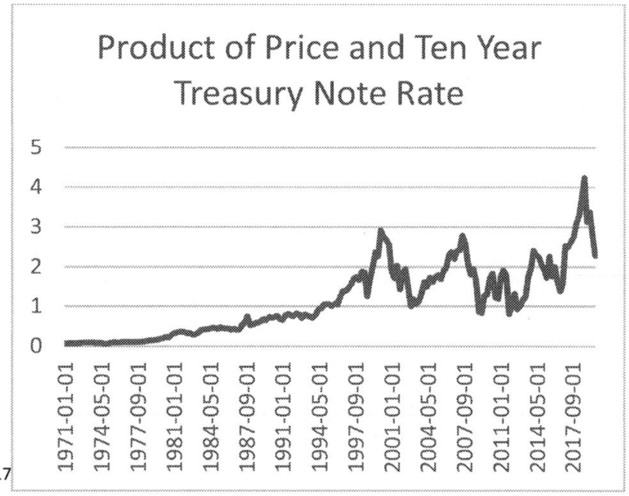

The product of the risk-free rate and price identifies both recent major market bubbles (2000 and 2007) as did the price to value ratio. However, unlike the price to value ratio, it accounts for the decrease in rates following 2018 and adjusts to reflects the relative decrease in expensiveness that results by decreasing the risk-free rate and increasing the attractiveness of risk-assets.

---

[16] Wilshire Associates, Wilshire 5000 Total Market Full Cap Index [WILL5000INDFC], retrieved from FRED, Federal Reserve Bank of St. Louis; https://fred.stlouisfed.org/series/WILL5000INDFC, November 21, 2019.

[17] Wilshire Associates, Wilshire 5000 Total Market Full Cap Index [WILL5000INDFC], retrieved from FRED, Federal Reserve Bank of St. Louis; https://fred.stlouisfed.org/series/WILL5000INDFC, November 21, 2019. U.S. Bureau of Economic Analysis, Gross Domestic Product [GDP], retrieved from FRED, Federal Reserve Bank of St. Louis; https://fred.stlouisfed.org/series/GDP, November 21, 2019.

The product of price and the risk-free rate, however, has a critical failure in that it fails to appropriately scale increases in productive value (since that is not an input in its function). As a result, it has a tendency to misprice the relative expensiveness of historic highs relative to one another.

As an example, the product of price and the risk-free rate identifies the expensiveness of 2000 and 2007 as being nearly identical (although on the price to value ratio, it is clear that the market was actually more expensive in 2000 than in 2007). Similarly, the product of the price and the risk-free rate overstates the expensiveness of the market in 2016 until 2018, because it fails to account for increases in price which result from the per unit increase in productive value added to the U.S. economy during the same period (coupled with the combined effects of an increase in prices coupled with a gradual rate hiking policy by the federal reserve during that time period).

As a result, the product of the price and the risk-free rate provides an inferior measure of relative market expense than the Formula which accounts for per unit increases/decreases in productive value together with movement in the risk-free rate.

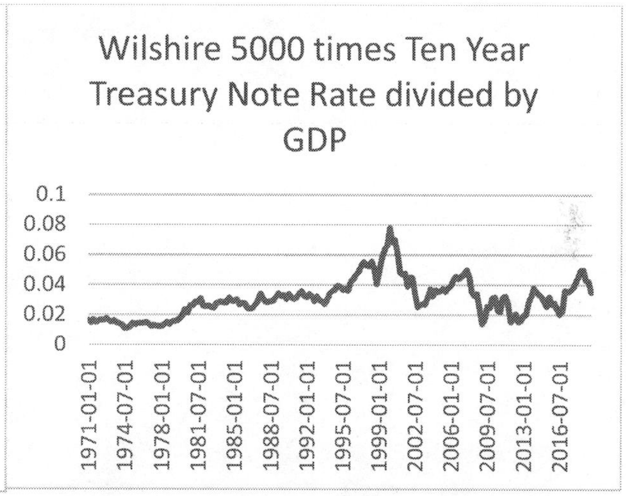

Despite the superiority of the Formula, it is important to note that the underlying components ratios are useful and should be monitored. By way of example, it is easier to spot inflation or deflation through a chart of the risk-free rate alone. It is easiest to spot the effect of inflation and deflation (or interest rate moves generally) on price using a chart of the product of price and the risk-free rate alone. Similarly, it is easier to determine the nominal price being paid per unit of value received using price to value alone (which may be extremely helpful to know if an investor is seeking to compound returns on free cashflow paid from investments). However, for a holistic view of relative market expense, the Formula is superior to either the product of price and the risk-free rate or the price to value ratio alone.

To be clear, neither the product of the price and risk-free rate or price to value ratio are inherently flawed. They simply do not account for the entirety of the factors which affect asset pricing. That is to say, value is not the only component of price (although it is a major component). Similarly, the risk-free rate is not the only component of price (although it is also a major component). Together, however, accounting for the two largest contributors to price, provides a superior formula with the ability to identify relative expense on the basis of the aggregation of price to value and risk-adjusted price. By nature of this aggregation, the Formula provides a superior historical ratio which can be used as an effective point of comparison.

Historical Performance

To confirm the consistency and accuracy of the Formula, it is helpful to review historical data.

While, in my view the Wilshire 5000 is generally speaking a better proxy for the price of the total U.S. equity market, to provide a more robust dataset it is helpful to look to the S&P index (which as a total market index serves reasonably well to approximate total market price).

While the prior analysis was quarterly, historical analysis will be yearly to account for the large size of the dataset.

1871 to Present

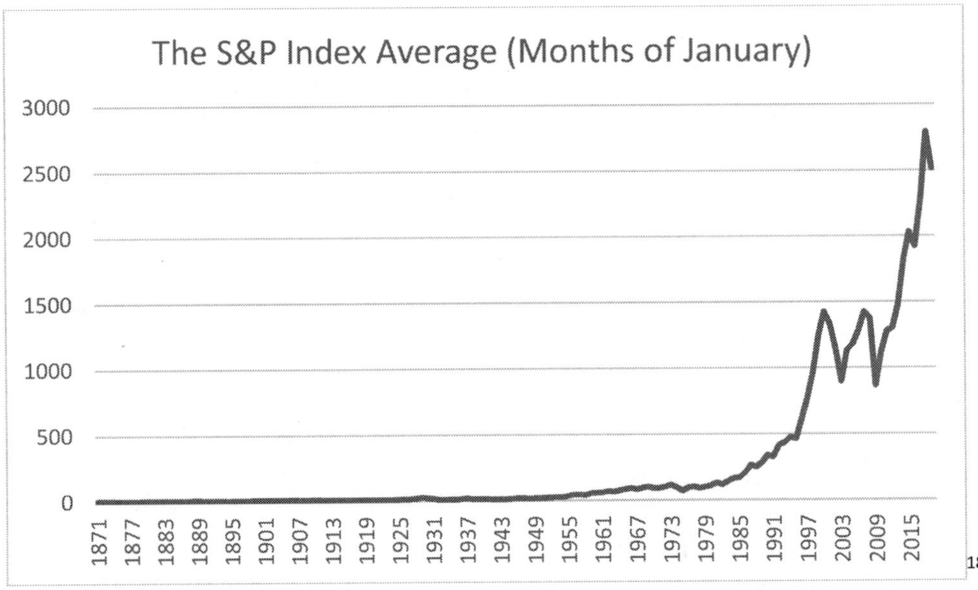

[18]

Beginning first with price, it is clear that since 1871 the price of the S&P index (and the overall market capitalization of the U.S. stock market) has increased steadily with time.

---

[18] https://www.multpl.com/s-p-500-historical-prices/table/by-month

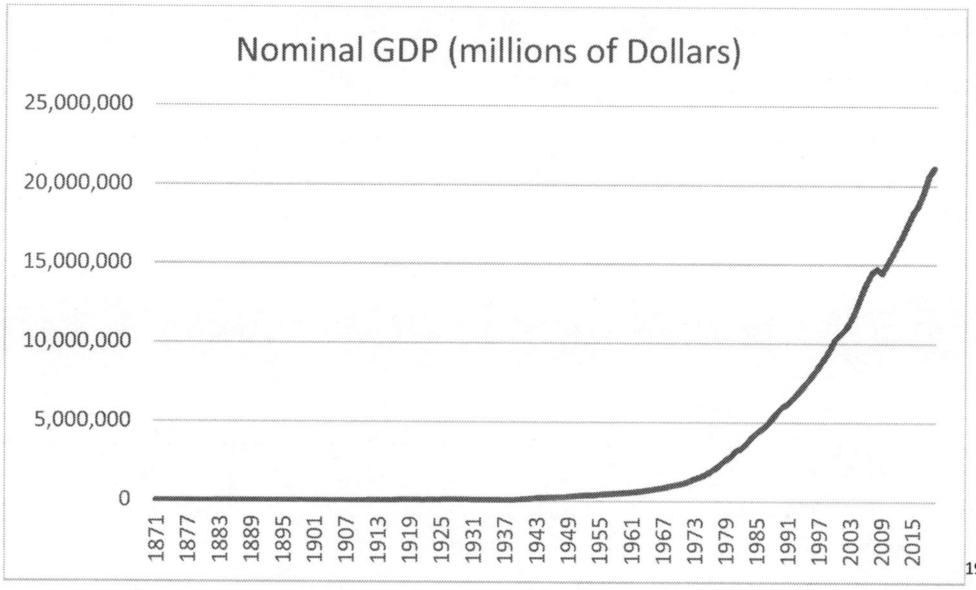

[19]

Looking next at value, it is clear that the productive value of the U.S. economy has increased steadily with time in proportion to the increase in price (more accurately price has increased in proportion with the increase in value, but the point is the same).

The proportion by which price has increased in accordance with increased productive value is evidenced by the ratio of price to value. From the chart above, it is clear that since the 1870s the productive value of the U.S. economy has increased at a faster rate than the corresponding increase in price. Said another way, the price per unit of value of the U.S. economy has steadily decreased with time (despite the high increase in the overall price of the U.S. marketplace). This is most likely due to productive

[19] Louis Johnston and Samuel H. Williamson, "What Was the U.S. GDP Then?" MeasuringWorth, 2019. http://www.measuringworth.org/usgdp/

innovation and structural changes in the U.S. economy, the U.S. system of government and monetary supply.[20]

[21]

Looking next at the ten-year treasury note rate, it is clear that the risk-free rate oscillated, but was fairly consistent from 1871 onward until the 1970s, when a great inflation occurred which lasted until the early 1980s (as evidenced by the historic spike in interest rates). Following the great inflation, the risk-free rate has steadily decreased until the present time.

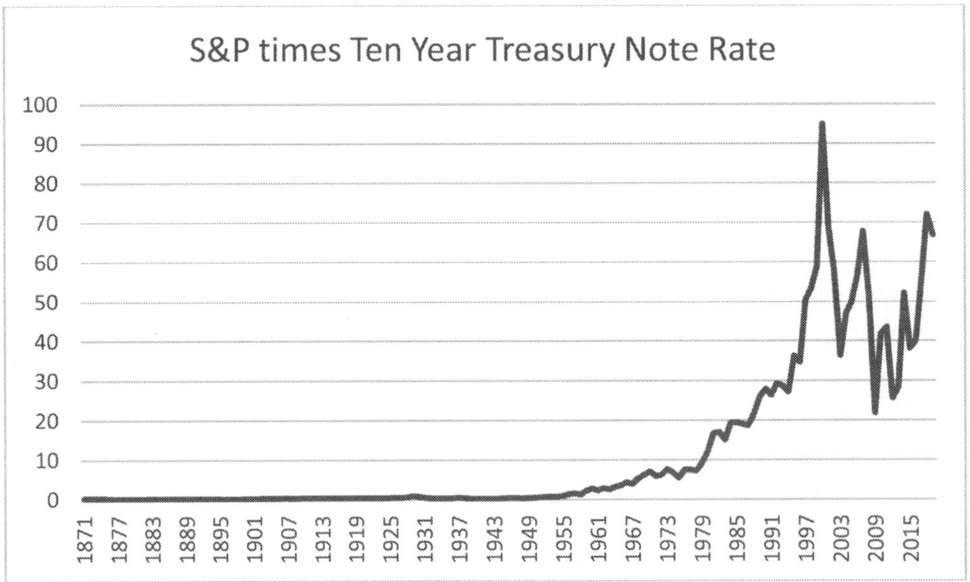

Looking at the product of the S&P and the ten-year treasury note rate, it is clear that the dramatic increase in price over time has significantly distorted the scale of the chart. Despite this distortion,

[20] It is notable that during this period of time the U.S. transformed from an agrarian economy to an industrial and ultimately service economy.

[21] https://www.multpl.com/10-year-treasury-rate/table/by-year

however, it is still clear that deflation or a decreasing risk-free rate had the effect of decreasing relative expensiveness despite significant increases in price over the same period (as an example the nominal price of the S&P in 1997 was nearly the same in 2007, yet deflation/lower risk-free rates result in a much lower "expensiveness" reading. Similarly, despite price more than doubling from the high set in 2007, the current market is of only relative similar expense to the high set in 2007 (according to this chart) because of the corresponding decrease in the risk-free rate over the period.

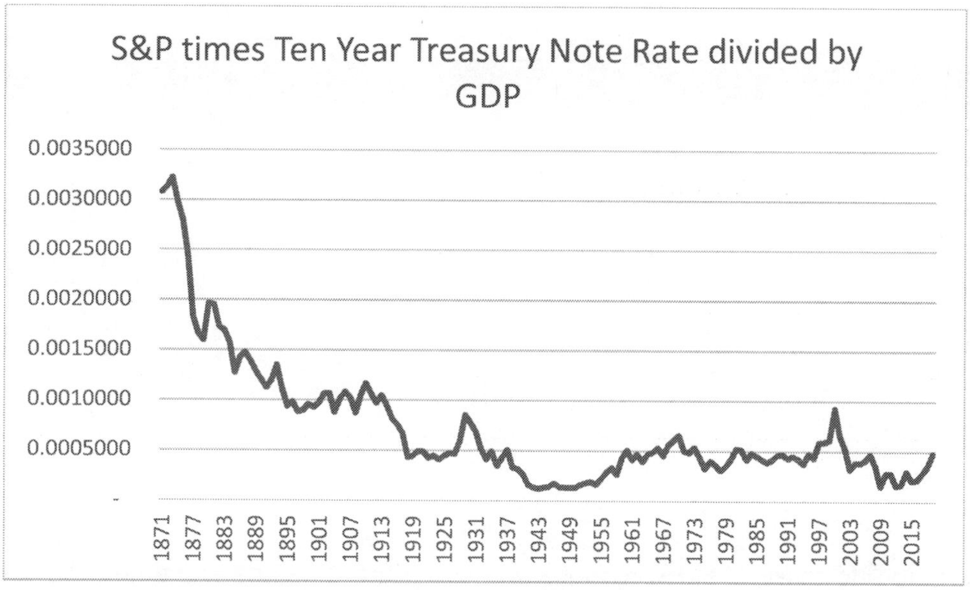

Looking now at the Formula, it is clear that the relative expense of the U.S. economy steadily decreased from the 1870s until the early 1900s. Looking back at the price to value ratio and the product of the price and risk-free rate, it seems clear that this decrease in relative expense is due to the decrease in the price per unit of production in the U.S. economy that was experienced over the period (during this time interest rates oscillated but remained relatively constant and are therefore unlikely to have significantly contributed to the relative decrease in the expense of the U.S. economy).

Since the 1900s (when the U.S. economy more or less took its modern form) through the present, the relative expense of the U.S. economy has remained relatively constant (oscillating within standard deviations around a historic mean).

Taking a closer look now at 1915 through the present a number of factors become particularly clear.

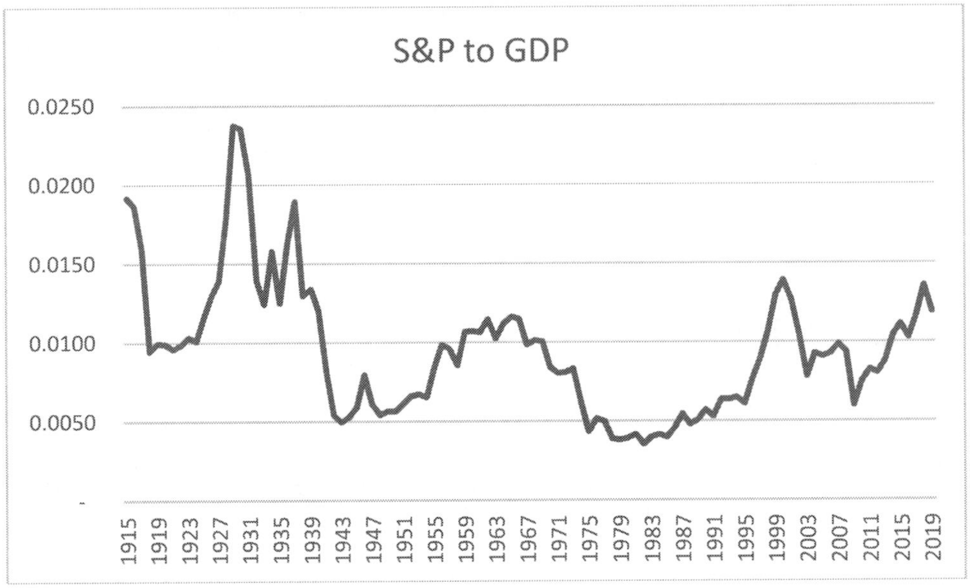

First, on a price to value basis, the U.S. economy was severely overvalued four times over the past approximately 100 years. Those years are 1929 (the Great Depression), 1960 to 1970 (the Great Inflation), 2000 (the Dot-Com bubble) and 2018 (the prior year). During the years since 1915, the historical average price to value ratio was 0.0095 with a standard deviation of 0.0045. Since 1915 the price to value ratio has been beyond one standard deviation above the historical mean ratio over the following time periods, 1928 to 1936, 2000 and 2018. Since 1915 the price to value ratio has ranged within one standard deviation below the historical mean ratio over the following time periods, 1943 to 1954, 1975 to 1995 and 2009 (representing periods of under-valuation).

[22]

Second, interest rates remained stable between 1915 until the early 1960s when they increased dramatically (correspondingly with inflation) until 1982. In 1982, the inflationary cycle peaked and the risk-free rate steadily declined (correspondingly with deflation) reaching a historic low in 2011. Over these periods, movement in the risk-free rate from 1915 until the early 1960s is unlikely to have impacted the relative expense of the market. From the 1960s until 1982, increases in the risk-free rate had the effect of increasing the relative expensiveness of the market. From 1982 through the present, a declining risk-free rate has had the effect of decreasing the relative expense of the market.

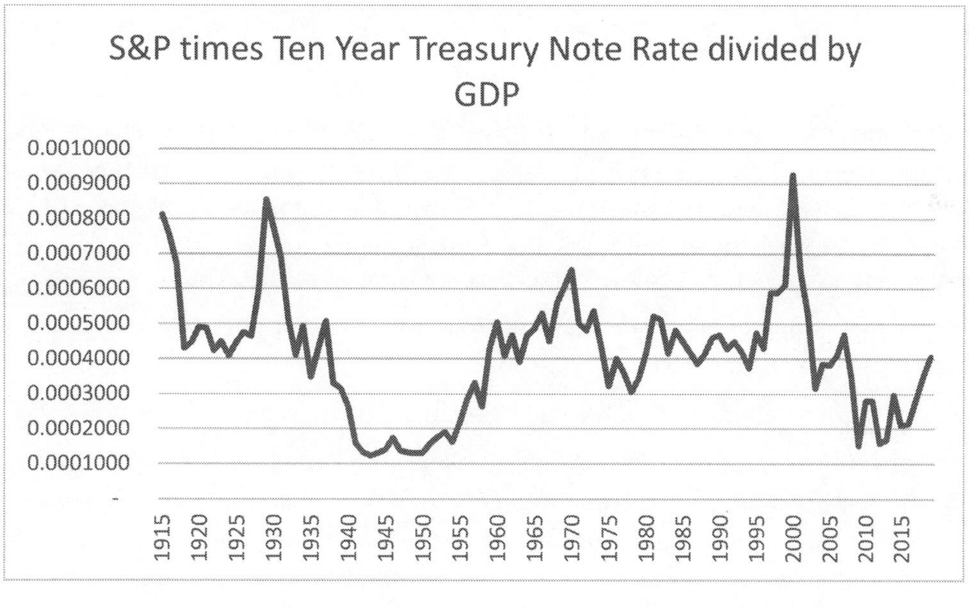

Considering price to value and the risk-free rate together through the Formula, a number of interesting observations become clear.

[22] https://www.multpl.com/10-year-treasury-rate/table/by-year

First, the Formula data provides a historical average of 0.004 with a standard deviation of 0.0017. Readings two standard deviations above the mean have only occurred three times since 1915: 1928-1932 (the Great Depression), 1969 to 1971 (the Great Inflation) and 1998-2002 (the Dot-Com Bubble). Clearly identifiable peaks during these periods occur in 1929, 1970 and 2000 respectfully. Two standard deviations below the mean have only occurred twice since 1915: 1941-1954 (WWII and Post-WWII recovery) and 2009-2016 (Financial Crisis and Post-Crisis recovery). Readings of one standard deviation above and below the mean occur more frequently since 1915 corresponding with "smaller" crises/recessions and booms/bubbles.

Second, the values of the Formula and the price to value ratio are clearly correlated[23]. However, the chart is noticeably different in a few areas.

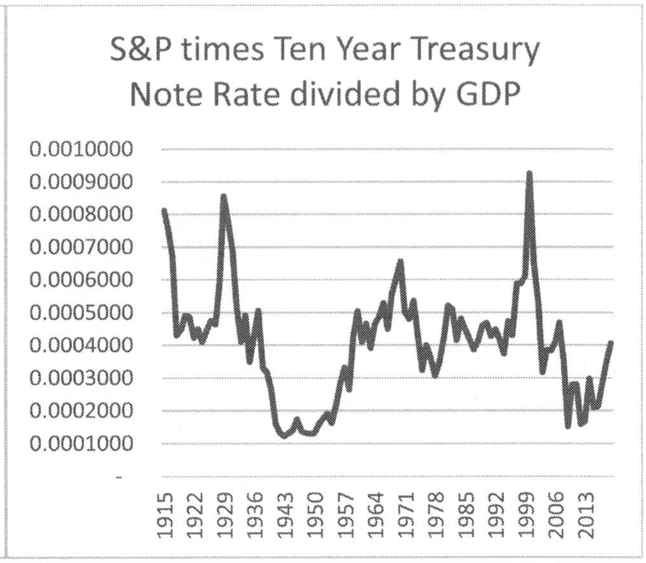

The Formula and price to value differ most obviously in the scaling of various over- and under-pricing. By way of example, looking first at the price to value ratio, the ratio suggests that the market was most overvalued in 1929 (leading up to the Great Depression) and has not achieved expense of that historic level since. 1970, 2000 and 2018 all achieve similar historic expense levels, but not on an order of magnitude equivalent to 1929 on a price to value basis. Conversely, the Formula provides two moments in history of equal magnitude of expense: 1929 and 2000 (with 1970 slightly less expensive in magnitude although clearly significantly expensive).

This variance in magnitude is a direct result of the difference in interest rates during the periods. By way of example, in 1929 the ten-year treasury note rate was 3.60%. During 2000 the ten-year treasury note rate was 6.66% (roughly double the risk-free rate in 1929). Thus, while the nominal price per unit of value in the 1920s was significantly higher (roughly double) than during the Dot-com bubble; on a risk-adjusted basis, the Dot-com bubble was moderately more expensive on a per unit basis than the 1929 market given in 1929 the risk-free rate would yield only half the rate of return an investor could achieve risk free in 2000.

[23] A calculated Pearson's coefficient of 0.58 indicating strong correlation.

To be clear there is no harm in using price-to-value as a barometer of relative expense since it provides consistent points of comparison over time, however, price-to-value lacks the precision of accounting for the risk-free rate in making historical comparisons.

Before moving on, it is important to note that neither a price to value ratio nor the Formula are intended as market timing devices. That is to say, their utility is not in forecasting the timing of recessions, but rather to indicate relative expense at any given time. Generally speaking, one can expect to enjoy superior returns from purchasing an asset during times of relative cheapness and to suffer through inferior returns from purchasing an asset during times of relative expense. The Formula, however, is more precise than a simple price per unit of value metric, because it "risk-adjusts", i.e. attributes the price per unit value metric to the risk-free rate of return in making a determination of "risk-adjusted" expense. I will note, however, that market tops are typically associated with relative over-expensiveness on a historic basis as evidenced by the historical data.[24]

[24] By way of example, if you purchased equities during the 2000 height of the dot-com bubble, 10 years later (on a purely priced based metric) your return would be approximately 0%. Conversely, if you purchased equities during the height of the run-up to the 2009 financial crisis your return 10 years later (once again purely considering price appreciation) would be approximately 100%. A price to value metric would have indicated both events of being the same historic expensiveness, whereas the returns achieved thereafter clearly indicate that the historic expense of 2000 clearly exceeded the expensiveness of the run-up to 2009. On a pure investment decision basis, however, it would probably be wise to avoid the relative expensiveness of both 2000 and the run-up to 2009 to enhance returns.

Statistical Considerations

Based on the historical data reviewed, there are a number of important statistical considerations that should be addressed.

First, the relationships noted above carry statistical significance. Using the historical S&P data discussed as an example, it is notable that:

1) Price and value are correlated with a Pearson coefficient of 0.96. Indicating near perfect statistical correlation. This makes sense inherently since value is the fundamental component of calculating price for any asset. As a result, changes in value have a strong and immediate effect on pricing.
2) Price and the risk-free rate are inversely correlated with a Pearson coefficient of -0.16. This too makes inherent sense since the same per unit price is more attractive when the risk-free rate is low then when the risk-free rate is high. Thus, increases in the risk-free rate negatively impact price and decreases in the risk-free rate positively impact price. It should also be noted that the correlation between price and the risk-free rate is far less significant than the correlation between price and value.
3) The product of price and the risk-free rate and price are correlated with a Pearson coefficient of 0.88. The variance in the coefficient (from 1.00 being price correlated to price) resulting from the risk-free rate being included in the product.
4) The price to value ratio and price are not significantly correlated with a Pearson coefficient of 0.05. This makes inherent sense because expensiveness is not necessarily tied to nominal purchase price.
5) The price to value ratio and the Formula are correlated with a Pearson coefficient of 0.58 indicating moderate to strong correlation. The variance between the price to value ratio and the Formula is attributable to the inclusion of the risk-free rate.
6) The risk-free rate and the Formula are mildly correlated with a Pearson coefficient of 0.38. The variance between the risk-free rate and the Formula being attributable to the inclusion of the price to value ratio in the Formula.

Log Values and Scaling

It is worth noting that the scale of the ratios provided herein can be scaled through the use of logarithmic distribution or through scaling of component datasets. As a matter of mathematics, altering base-ten scale will not alter the historical relationship of ratio values (or correlations among these values if consistently applied) beyond the scale with which they are reported in proportion to the scale used (although the ratio values themselves will change). For purposes of the S&P nominal GDP has been scaled in hundreds of millions of U.S. dollars, but one is free to normalize values of datasets as they see fit.

Mathematical Operation of the Formula

As can be seen from the correlations, the Formula operates by taking price multiplying by an inversely correlated factor influencing price and dividing the product by a correlated factor. Increases in the numerator will increase the ratio (through the increase in price or increase in the inversely correlated risk-free rate) and decreases in the numerator will decrease the ratio (through the decrease in price or decrease in the inversely correlated risk-free rate). Increases in the denominator (resulting from increases in value) will decrease the ratio and decreases in the denominator (resulting from decreases in value) will increase the ratio. This mathematical relationship has the effect of increasing the ratio when price increases, the risk-free rate increases or value decreases and decreasing the ratio when price decreases, the risk-free rate decreases or value increases. A high ratio value is indicative of expensiveness and a low value ratio is indicative of cheapness. Said simply in financial terms, the Formula is the price per unit of value multiplied by the risk-free rate of return.

Forecasting

Beyond simply being a consistent measure of history, the Formula provides a few key insights.

1) A lower-risk free rate supports prices while a higher-risk free rate contributes to relative expensiveness of risk assets

As seen in the discussion of 1915 to the present, lowering the risk-free rate increases the attractiveness of risk-assets and supports higher price per unit of value. Conversely raising the risk-free rate decreases the attractiveness of risk-assets and supports lower price per unit value. This is consistent with the Capital Asset Pricing Model and the fact that, in stable modern economies, the risk-free rate moves primarily in accordance with expectations of inflation or deflation.

2) Increases in productive value support higher prices, while decreases in productive value depress prices

As seen in the discussion of 1915 to the present, increases in productive value decrease price per unit of value, while decreases in productive value increase price per unit of value. Thus, increased value supports higher prices and decreased value supports lower prices.

3) Rational increases in prices are supported by increases in productive value or decreases in the risk-free rate, while rational decreases in prices result from decreases in productive value or increases in the risk-free rate.

As seen in the discussion of 1915 to the present, increases in price tend to be supported by either increases in productive value or decreases in the risk-free rate or some combination thereof. An increase in productive value in an increasing risk-free rate environment minimizes the impact of the increased productive value on price. An increase in productive value in a decreasing risk-free rate environment increases the magnitude of the impact of increased productive value of price. A decrease in the risk-free rate in an environment of decreasing productive value minimizes the impact of the decreasing productive value on price. An increase in the risk-free rate in an environment of decreasing productive value exacerbates the impact of the decreasing productive value on price.[25]

4) The relative expensiveness of the economic system stays fairly consistent over time.

As seen in the discussion of 1915 to the present, despite vast increases in the nominal value of equities, significant swings in the risk-free rate and vast increases in the productive value of the U.S. economy, the relative expense of the economic system remained fairly consistent over the last 100+ years. That is to say, the ratio of the relative expense of the U.S. economy tends to remain within two standard deviations of a historical mean value. Two standard deviations over the mean tends to indicate extreme expense and two standard deviations below the mean tends to indicate extreme cheapness.

Given these insights, one can make a number of determinations.

---

[25] A natural logical inference from this discussion is that price increases or decreases which cannot be accounted for by proportional changes in the aggregation of forces of productive value and movement in the risk-free rate are a result of market "irrationality" (i.e. misguided expectations of future earnings or misguided sentiment toward an asset, market or economy).

1) The ratio value can be compared against the historical average to make a determination of relative expense.

Because of the relative consistency of ratio values historically and consistent distribution around a historic mean value, one can compare current calculations of the ratio to prior ratio values throughout history to determine whether the asset, market or economy to be purchased is historically expensive.

2) Using a set ratio value, one can calculate the value of any of the 3 variables provided the other two are known.

Using simple algebraic expression, it is possible to determine a hypothetical value or range of values if a ratio value is known or set and the remaining variables remain constant. As an example, the Formula $R_v = (P \times R_f) / V$ can be expressed as $R_f = (R_v \times V)/P$. Using real figures as an example, a ratio value of 0.006 (which would represent historic expense of a magnitude observed in the Dot-com bubble or Great Depression), January 2019's S&P price of 2,510.03 and January 2019's nominal GDP print of 210,988.27 (in hundreds of millions), one can calculate a ten-year treasury note rate of 3.41%.[26]

By using present day values (November 21, 2019) as set forth below as an example, one could make a variety of forecasts.

$R_v = (P \times R_f) / V$

$R_v = 0.003$

$P = 3{,}103.54$

$R_f = 1.78$ (as of November 21, 2019)

$V = 21{,}525.82$ (as of October 30, 2019)

Where the ratio value of 0.003 represents roughly one standard deviation below the historical mean value of 0.004.

If we assume, however, a historic ratio value of **0.006** or approximately two standard deviations above the mean (which would indicate historic expense on par with 1929 and 2000), we can infer the following:

If price and value are held constant the risk-free rate is **4.16%**. Said another way, if price and value were to stay constant and the ten-year treasury note rate rose to 4.16%, the ratio would indicate historic expense.

If price and the risk-free rate are held constant, value is **9,207.17**. This would indicate a 57% drop in GDP. Said another way, it would take a 57% drop in GDP to reach historic expense levels, if price and the risk-free rate remained constant.[27]

---

[26] As we know, the true ten-year treasury note rate was 2.66% in January 2019, but our ability to forecast indicates that all things being equal a ten-year treasury note rate up to 3.41% could have been supported before historic expense would have occurred (admittedly extreme expense consistent with economic calamity).

[27] While this is true mathematically, because of the near perfect correlation between price and value, in reality, a drop in value of this magnitude would likely cause market hysteria and an extreme decline in prices. After accounting for the correlation coefficient between price and value a decline in GDP of 2.28% would be sufficient to

If value and the risk-free rate are held constant, price could be as high as **7,255.89**. This would indicate a 134% increase in price from today's close. Said another way, it would take a 134% increase in price from today's close to reach historic expense levels, if price and the risk-free rate remained constant.

If we assume, however a historic ratio value of 0.005 or approximately one standard deviation above the mean (which would indicate expense on par with 2007), we can infer the following:

If price and value are held constant the risk-free rate could be as high as **3.47%**. Said another way, if price and value were to stay constant and the ten-year treasury rate rose to 3.47%, the ratio would indicate historic expense consistent with the period leading up to the 2007-2009 financial crisis.

If price and the risk-free rate are held constant, value could drop as far as **11,048.60**. This would indicate a 49% drop in GDP. Said another way, it would take a 49% drop in GDP to reach historic expense levels, if price and the risk-free rate remained constant.[28]

If value and the risk-free rate are held constant, price could be as high as **6,046.58**. This would indicate a 95% increase in price from today's close. Said another way, it would take a 95% increase in price from today's close to reach historic expense levels, if price and the risk-free rate remained constant.

If we assume, a historic ratio value of 0.004, which is the historic mean and would indicate neutral historic market expense, we can infer the following:

If price and value are held constant the risk-free rate could be as high as **2.77%**. Said another way, if price and value were to stay constant and the ten-year treasury rate rose to 2.77%, the ratio would indicate historic expense consistent with the historic mean.

If price and the risk-free rate are held constant, value could drop as far as **13,810.75**. This would indicate a 36% drop in GDP. Said another way, it would take a 36% drop in GDP to reach historically average ratio levels, if price and the risk-free rate remained constant.[29]

If value and the risk-free rate are held constant, price could be as high as **4,837.26**. This would indicate a 56% increase in price from today's close. Said another way, it would take a 56% increase in price from today's close to reach historically average ratio levels, if value and the risk-free rate remained constant.

If we assume, a historic ratio value of 0.002, or approximately two standard deviations below the historic mean (which would indicate historic cheapness as seen in the 1940s and 2007), we can infer the following:

---

cause historic over-valuation. For purposes of the example, however, this more sophisticated analysis will be ignored for sake of simplicity.

[28] After accounting for the correlation coefficient between price and value a decline in GDP of 1.96% would be sufficient to cause historic over-valuation.

[29] After accounting for the correlation coefficient between price and value a decline in GDP of 1.44% would be sufficient to cause historic average-valuation.

If price and value are held constant the risk-free rate could be as low as **1.39%**. Said another way, if price and value were to stay constant and the ten-year treasury note rate dropped to 1.39%, the ratio would indicate historic cheapness consistent with the 1940s and 2007.

If price and the risk-free rate are held constant, value could rise as far as **27,621.51**. This would indicate a 28% increase in GDP. Said another way, it would take a 28% increase in GDP to reach historically cheap ratio levels, if price and the risk-free rate remained constant.[30]

If value and the risk-free rate are held constant, price could be as low as **2,418.63**. This would indicate a 22% decrease in price from today's close. Said another way, it would take a 22% decrease in price from today's close to reach historically cheap ratio levels, if price and the risk-free rate remained constant.

From the discussion above a few quick observations are worth noting, first, GDP tends to grow steadily in the U.S. at somewhere between 1% and 3% annually. Similarly, during periods of contraction GDP tends to contract within a range of 0 to -2.5%. As such, it is clear that rather than forecasting future value data based on relative expense, it makes most sense to hold GDP constant (or within a range of +/- 0-3%).[31] This additional stable point of reference, assists in making more accurate forecasts of price and/or the risk-free rate.

Given the stability of GDP[32], we can reasonably ascertain that:

It would take an increase in the risk-free rate to **4.16%** or a 134% increase in price to **7,255.89** to reach a historic ratio value of **0.006** or approximately two standard deviations above the mean (which would indicate historic expense on par with 1929 and 2000).

It would take an increase in the risk-free rate to **3.47%** or a 95% increase in price from today's close to **6,046.58** to reach a historic ratio value of **0.005** or approximately one standard deviation above the mean (which would indicate expense on par with 2007).

It would take an increase in the risk-free rate to **2.77%** or a 56% increase in price from today's close to **4,837.26** to reach a historic ratio value of **0.004** or the historic mean.

It would take a decrease in the risk-free rate to **1.39%** or a 22% decrease in price from today's close to **2,418.63** to reach a historic value of **0.002**, or approximately two standard deviations below the historic mean (which would indicate historic cheapness as seen in the 1940s and 2009).

---

[30] After accounting for the correlation coefficient between price and value an increase in GDP of 1.12% would be sufficient to cause historic under-valuation.

[31] "GDP growth (annual %) - United States." World Bank national accounts data, and OECD National Accounts data files. Retrieved from https://data.worldbank.org/indicator/NY.GDP.MKTP.KD.ZG?locations=US. November 21, 2019.

[32] Naturally any decrease or increase in GDP will move these figures, but for the purposes of explanation, we can assume stable GDP. It should also be noted that GDP is correlated 0.96 to price, such that changes in GDP tend to have an immediate and substantial impact on price so the calculations derived are not exactly precise. They do however provide a range of reference. A more complex equation would account for the correlated impact of factors (i.e. a 0.96 correlation coefficient for value and a -0.15 correlation coefficient for the risk-free rate).

The current risk-free rate (1.78%), price (3,103.54) and GDP (21,525.82) indicate a ratio of roughly 0.003 indicating one deviation below the historic mean of 0.004.

This forecast provides a few key insights:

First, because of the current ratio of 0.003 (which is one standard deviation below the 0.004 historical mean), the market is currently relatively under-valued on a risk-adjusted basis.

Second, an increase in the risk-free rate by as little as 238 basis points could put the equity markets in over-valued territory not seen since the Dot-com bubble or the Great Depression. This is particularly sobering considering the ten-year treasury note rate was as high as 3% two years ago. Similarly, a relatively small uptick in inflation expectations could easily drive the ten-year treasury note rate beyond 4%. Some financial professionals as recently as May of last year believed the ten-year treasury note rate should be roughly 4% and that such a rate "wouldn't be a bad thing".[33] From the model above, it seems clear that a 4% ratio would be a "bad thing" for the relative expense of the U.S. equity markets (and any associated expectations of equity returns).[34]

Third, a risk-free rate of around 2.77%, at current price and value levels, yields a ratio of 0.004, which is equivalent to the historical mean. On this basis we can infer that it is probable that the neutral rate for the current U.S. economy is somewhere between 2.50% and 3.00%. This suggests the Federal Reserve rate cutting policy is intended to allow the economy to run "hot" absent any significant inflation expectations.[35]

---

[33] Jamie Dimon, CEO of J.P. Morgan espoused a 4% rate as being "not a bad thing" as recently as May 2019 (such a rate would have caused a significant price deleveraging based on the model). Although to be fair a higher interest rate might conceivably be better for his bank even if it was bad for the global equity markets (it might also be better for the ultimate health of the U.S. economy to experience a deleveraging, although it seems unlikely Dimon was making that suggestion). https://www.bloomberg.com/news/articles/2019-05-08/dimon-says-u-s-yields-extraordinarily-low-prepare-for-change. It is notable however, that he has since reversed course and JP Morgan is preparing for 0% interest rates. https://www.cnbc.com/2019/09/10/jamie-dimon-says-jp-morgan-preparing-for-0percent-interest-rates-in-us.html

[34] While beyond the scope of the analysis, it would also be a dangerous thing to need to enter a rate hiking cycle to quell inflation, if equity prices were already falling together with GDP. Raising rates during such a period would effectively increase the risk-adjusted expensiveness of the market during a deleveraging, which would likely result in a deeper market correction than if the risk-free rate is lowered during the same period. Generally speaking, it is federal reserve policy to lower interest rates to combat recessions, the general consensus being it takes an approximately 400 basis point decrease to incentivize investment into risk-assets (or said another way, to decrease the risk-adjusted expensiveness of risk-assets sufficiently to make them attractive to investors).

[35] The spike in the ratio in late 2018 (which immediately preceded a 20% sell-off) also indicates the Federal Reserve hiked interest rates too far too quickly in its first attempt. It remains unclear whether this has already triggered a deleveraging that is already in progress (although the Federal Reserve has since reversed its rate hiking policy and returned to cutting rates).

Assumptions

It is worth mentioning that the forecasting analysis above makes a number of assumptions, which may or may not be true in the future.

First, it assumes that the historical distribution around a mean value of the ratio will continue in the future. This seems highly probable given the robust nature of the dataset (100+ years), but it is worth noting that if the U.S. economic or governmental system were to change drastically such that the price per unit of production changed dramatically, such a change could result in a new mean value and corresponding distribution. As an example, it is possible that innovations in cognitive computer-based learning or artificial intelligence so dramatically change the productive capability of the U.S. economy that the per unit price of production decreases in nature last seen in the early 1800s to early 1900s. Conversely, it is possible that the United States could adopt a different system of government or economic structure which either increases or decreases price per productive unit of output. If this were to be the case, one would expect a corresponding change in the historic distribution relative to the one experienced over the last 100+ years.

Second, it should be noted that while the various components of the Formula have been held stable while calculations of unknown values are made, it should be noted that in real time, all component variables of the Formula are likely to be moving and the magnitude by which they move relative to one another will be the determinant of ratio output. That is to say, it is highly probable that if GDP is rising, market prices will be rising and if GDP is falling market prices will be falling (although the magnitude by which price is rising/falling relative to value or vice versa will vary). Similarly, the risk-free rate is likely to move as prices and value are moving (in accordance with credit supply, inflation/deflation expectations and/or Federal Reserve policy). For purposes of analysis, however, holding variables constant while evaluating a single variable creates a range of outward-bounds which can be helpful in making expectations about the future.

Third, it is worth noting that forecasting is inherently speculative. The ratio will only produce results as accurate as the data which is input (the ubiquitous garbage in, garbage out). Thus, inaccurately forecasted data entries, will result in erroneous formula output. The mere fact GDP has exhibited historically stable growth does not mean it will necessarily do so in the future (although it seems likely). Similarly, the fact that inflation has been subdued over a long period of time, does not mean it will remain subdued in the future.[36] If one desired to forecast, however, the Formula would be useful in that one could effectively use a trend or linear regression analysis to provide input data for each variable of the Formula to generate a range of future expected risk-adjusted "expense" to determine if purchasing an asset, market or economy is wise in the present.[37]

It should be noted, however, for clarity that the Formula is not itself a forecasting device. It simply reports relative expense on a risk-free rate adjusted basis at any given time period for comparison with

---

[36] In fact, charts of the ten-year treasury note rate over the last 100+ seem to suggest that inflation/deflation and long-term credit cycles tend to last approximately 25-50 years. This is discussed more thoroughly in my book "Wayfinder: A Strategy for Navigating Financial Markets" by William DeCotiis.

[37] Additionally, other variables could certainly be added to the base formula for a more nuanced forecasting device, if desired.

historical norms. However, such comparison (and ranges which can be derived by mathematically manipulating the Formula) can provide a useful tool for informing policy makers and investors.

Fourth, the forecasting analysis discussed assumes that one's investment strategy or decision-making is made on the basis of risk-adjusted return. It may sound glib, but if an investor is not in the business of outperforming the market, is not in the business of using leverage, or is otherwise committed to an asset class without regard for the rate of return which could be generated safer elsewhere, then adjusting for the risk-free rate has limited value. In such case, a simple price to value ratio or similar metric will provide ample evidence of the relative expense or cheapness on a price per unit of production value basis.[38]

[38] As an example, it might be a perfectly reasonable position to take that paying double the price per unit of value is simply too expensive for one's investment portfolio regardless of the risk-free rate or whether such price is likely to be sustained. It is possible that ultra-long term investors who are not interested in out-performance, but rather slowly growing wealth overtime, might take this position on the basis movement in the risk-free rate cause "distortions" from true underlying "per unit" value and as such are to be ignored. This might particularly be the case if such investor is in the business of evaluating assets individually for inclusion in a portfolio based on individual investment cash returns (or if such investor primarily invests in assets in the form of cash since the benefit of cheaper available leverage will not assist in returns). Although for such investor, risk-adjusted price per unit will provide useful insight into why assets might seem unusually historically expensive for a sustained period (even if this won't impact investment or decision-making it is still helpful to know).

General Applicability Across Industries

While this paper has primarily discussed price, value and the risk-free rate in the context of equity markets, it is important to note that the Formula works for any dataset consisting of a price metric, a value metric and a risk-free (or standard rate), which are causally related. As a case study of the general applicability of the Formula, consider the housing market since 1991.[39]

[40]

Beginning first with price, it is clear from the chart above of nominal housing prices that home prices have steadily rose since 1992 despite a brief decline between 2007 and 2012 (corresponding with the housing crisis of 2009). In 2017 nominal housing prices increased beyond the nominal housing price experienced at the peak of the housing bubble in 2007. Without closer observation, an investor might be erroneously led to believe that because this pre-crisis level has been reached, home prices are "over-valued". This conclusion would be incorrect for a number of reasons.

---

[39] For two additional case studies please see Appendix A, Part I (Risk-adjusted CAPE Ratio) and Appendix A, Part II (Apple Stock Risk-adjusted PE).

[40] S&P Dow Jones Indices LLC, S&P/Case-Shiller U.S. National Home Price Index [CSUSHPINSA], retrieved from FRED, Federal Reserve Bank of St. Louis; https://fred.stlouisfed.org/series/CSUSHPINSA, November 21, 2019.

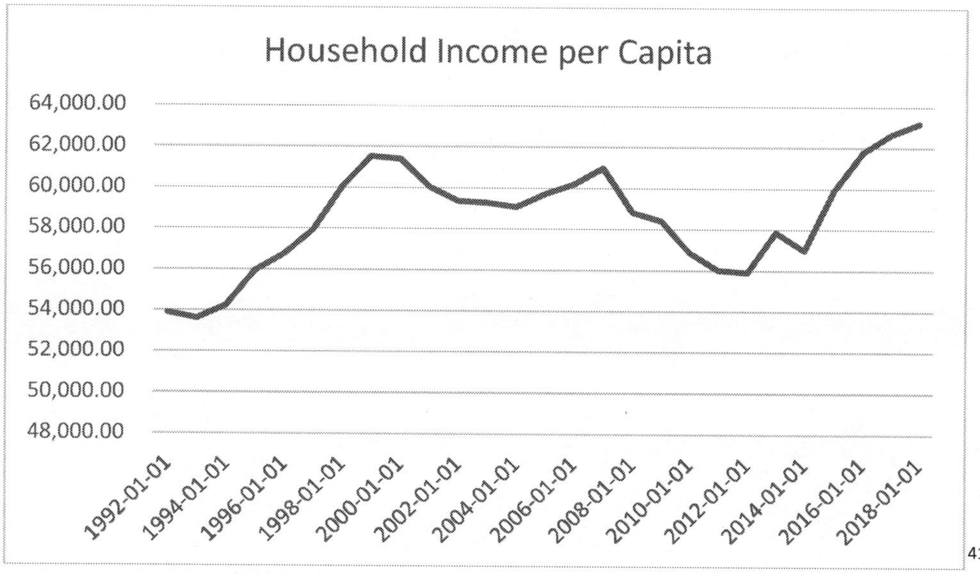

[41]

First, household income per capita has risen steadily since 2012 exceeding pre-crisis levels. However, just eyeballing the nominal housing price and per capita income doesn't provide sufficient detail into the magnitude by which each has increased relative to the other. To make such determination one looks to the price to value ratio.

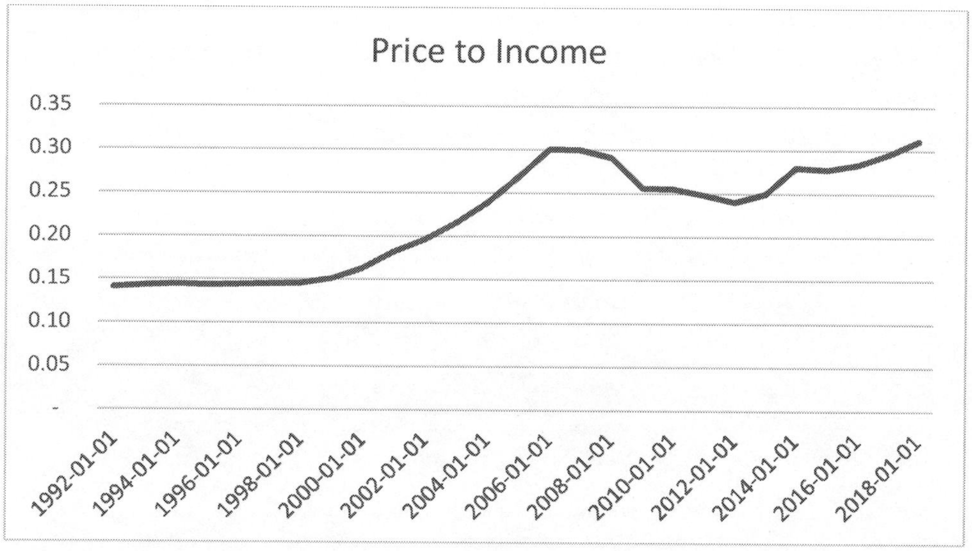

Dividing nominal housing price by household income per capita shows that while prices have increased so too have the income (and thereby the purchasing power) of households. However, as of 2017, the price to value ratio has exceeded the pre-crisis high ratio of 0.30. So is there a housing bubble?

[41] U.S. Census Bureau, Real Median Household Income in the United States [MEHOINUSA672N], retrieved from FRED, Federal Reserve Bank of St. Louis; https://fred.stlouisfed.org/series/MEHOINUSA672N, November 21, 2019.

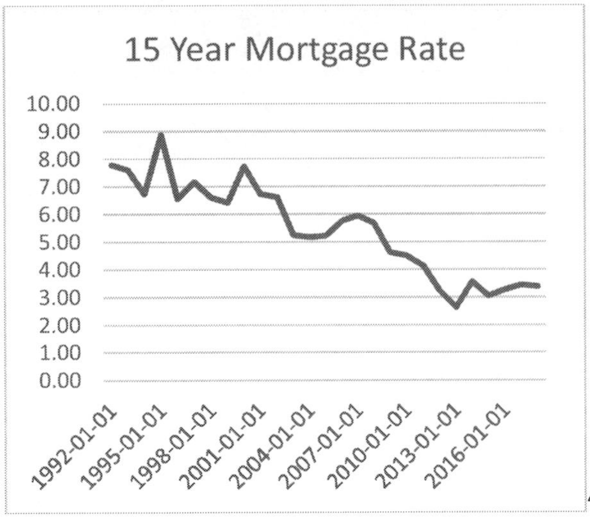

[42]

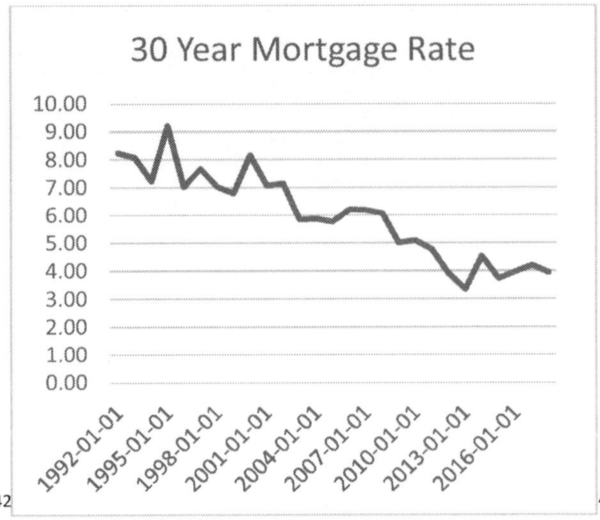

[43]

The price to value ratio does not account for the fact that both 15-year and 30-year mortgage rates (the most common types of mortgages) have steadily declined since 1992. This decrease in rates makes mortgages easier to service (by reducing the "cost" of the loan) and thereby makes homes easier to afford per unit of income.

As you can see from the charts of price/income x 15-year fixed mortgage rate and price/income x 30-year fixed mortgage rate, the relative expense of purchasing a home in 2007 (the pre-housing crisis high) far exceeded the relative expense of purchasing a home today. In fact, the magnitude of the decrease in the cost of mortgages (i.e. the decline in mortgage rates) was so substantial that the relative expense of purchasing a home since 2010 is analogous to purchasing a home in the early 1990s.

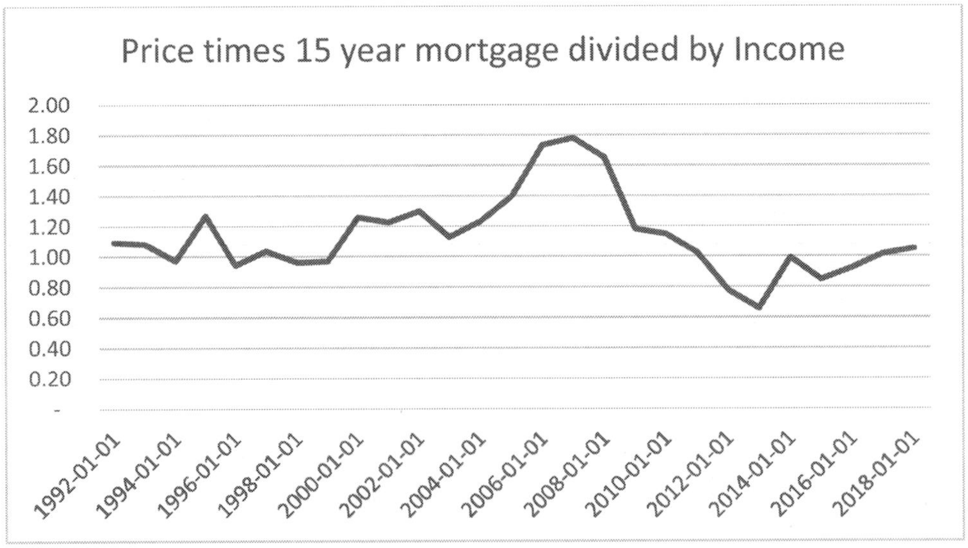

[42] Freddie Mac, 15-Year Fixed Rate Mortgage Average in the United States [MORTGAGE15US], retrieved from FRED, Federal Reserve Bank of St. Louis; https://fred.stlouisfed.org/series/MORTGAGE15US, November 21, 2019.
[43] Freddie Mac, 30-Year Fixed Rate Mortgage Average in the United States [MORTGAGE30US], retrieved from FRED, Federal Reserve Bank of St. Louis; https://fred.stlouisfed.org/series/MORTGAGE30US, November 21, 2019.

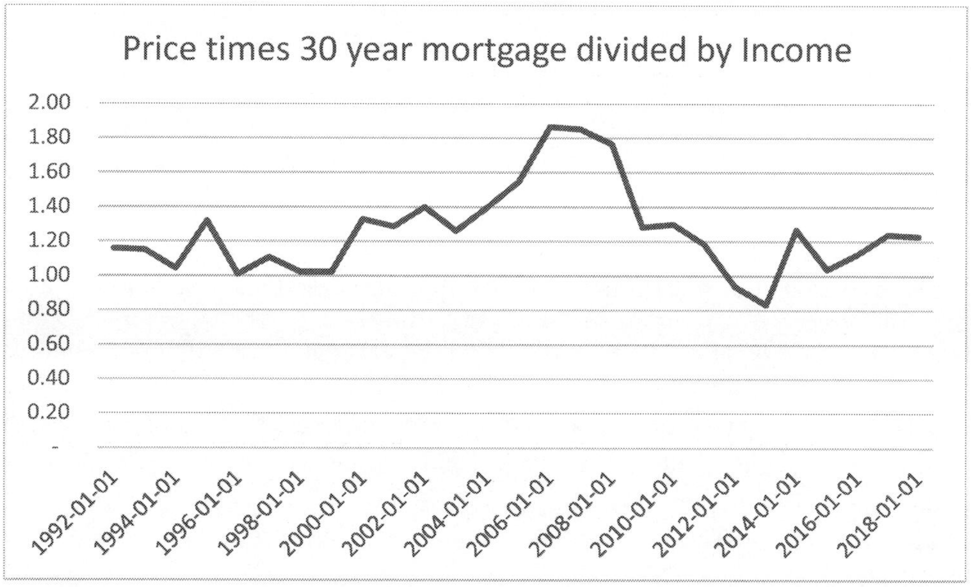

Thus, while the price to value ratio might suggest a housing bubble was afoot, adjusting for the relative cost of credit indicates that housing prices are actually reasonably valued. The danger of such analysis of course is that it relies on the relatively volatile mortgage rate to be sustained. That is to say, mortgage rates tend to be pegged to the risk-free rate and the risk-free rate tends to move in accordance with inflation/deflation expectations, central bank/government policy and credit market liquidity, any of which can easily change given the right conditions (additionally the premium of a mortgage rate over the risk-free rate also tends to move in accordance with certain factors adding additional volatility).

From the analysis above it is clear that if all other variables are held constant (i.e. if price and household income are held constant), an increase in 15-year mortgage rates to 5.73% and 30-year mortgage rates to 5.95% would put the housing market back at pre-crisis (housing bubble) levels (1.78, equivalent to the peak ratio of 2007, for the 15-year mortgage rate and 1.85, equivalent to the peak ratio of 2007, for the 30-year mortgage rate).

This is once again a sobering observation considering it would take a mere 2.00% increase to cause historic overvaluation in housing prices.[44]

[44] It is notable that the estimated increase in mortgage rates required to cause historic overvaluation is consistent with the 238 basis point estimated increase which would cause U.S. equity markets to become significantly overvalued. Such a coincidence seems to suggest that if the Federal Reserve policy were to cause interest rates to rise approximately 200 basis points from current levels a variety of seemingly unrelated markets across the U.S. economy would likely reach historic levels of over-valuation.

Pitfalls and Criticism

Despite the analysis of over-valuation above, it is important to identify limitations in the Formula promulgated.

First, the Formula is not a "market-timing device", it does not and cannot identify market tops with definitiveness. As an example, from the data compiled above it is not possible to determine whether 2018 marks a pre-recession peak market expense or will be surpassed once again in this business cycle.

Second, the Formula does not speak to the "overall health" of the asset, market or economy it measures. As an example, it may not be healthy for an already levered enterprise to take on additional debt because servicing costs have dropped, even though formulaically this would have the effect of decreasing relative expensiveness and supporting price in the short-term. The Formula is amoral in this sense and requires a certain nimbleness on the part of the observer to be useful (especially considering the speed with which the risk-free rate can move). The Formula does, however, identify relative expense at any given time.

A Speculative View Drawn from the Data

It is my general speculation that we are nearing the end of a long-term credit/deflationary cycle and that sooner or later inflation will take hold causing an uptick in the risk-free rate. When that occurs, if there has not been a meaningful increase in the production value of the U.S., it is likely that such uptick in rates will cause a meaningful price correction. The timing of this event is not clear. By treading carefully, the central bank could effectively maintain asset prices for some time to come. Perhaps a particularly clever central bank, could orchestrate maintaining rates just low enough just long enough to allow productive value to increase such that there is sufficient leeway to raise rates into future inflation. This seems unlikely, but is possible. Similarly, it is possible inflation never takes hold and we continue to live in a low rate deflationary world. This too seems unlikely as prolonged deflation and high levels of credit extension have always led to inflation historically (as evidenced by 25-50 year cycles of inflation/deflation and long-term credit cycles), it is, however, possible (albeit highly improbable).

What is clear, however, is that in the most recent business cycle, movement in the risk-free rate has been critically important to supporting asset prices. At current value and rates, price can be supported, however, as little as a 200 basis point increase could cause price correction. Additionally, because credit tends to be a part of asset pricing across the board, as little as a 200 basis point increase in the risk-free rate could have a price correcting impact on various assets, markets and economies (even if they appear superficially unrelated). This leaves the Federal Reserve and policy makers living on the very edge of a dangerous precipice as the U.S. economy flirts with disaster.

Conclusion

Regardless of my speculation, however, what is clear is that a ratio which incorporates the risk-free rate (or a standard rate) provides a more effective measure of historical value than a mere price to value ratio and provides an effective tool for policy makers and investors in making economic and investment decisions.

Appendix A

Part I (Risk-Adjusted CAPE)

As a case study of the general applicability of the Formula, consider cyclically-adjusted price to earnings (CAPE) since 1872.

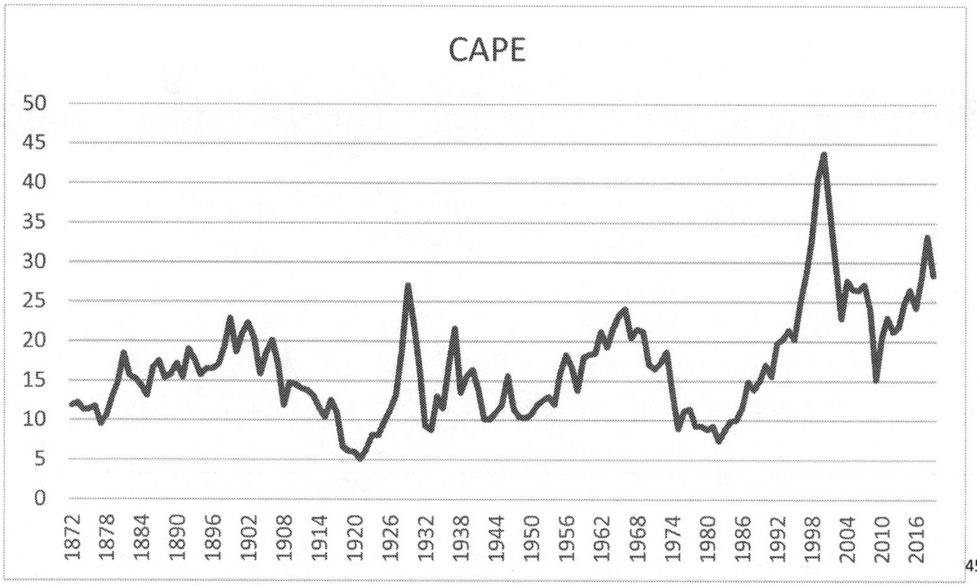

[45]

The CAPE ratio provides a fairly consistent measure of market expense over time. Because it is inflation adjusted and earnings are smoothed over a ten-year period, short-term volatility in price to earnings ratios and distortions resulting from inflation are eliminated making it a superior metric to a simple price to value ratio (price to earnings as an example). Since 1872 the historic mean for the CAPE ratio is 16.72 with a standard deviation of 6.75 (indicating over-valuation at a ratio of 23.47 and under-valuation at a ratio of 9.997). Based on one standard deviation from the mean, the chart of the CAPE ratio since 1872, identifies historic expensiveness in 1901-1902, 1929, 1937, 1966, 1998 – 2007 and 2017-present. The chart of the CAPE ratio since 1872 identifies historic inexpensiveness in 1915-1925, 1932-1933, 1943, 1949, and 1975-1985.

[45] https://www.multpl.com/shiller-pe

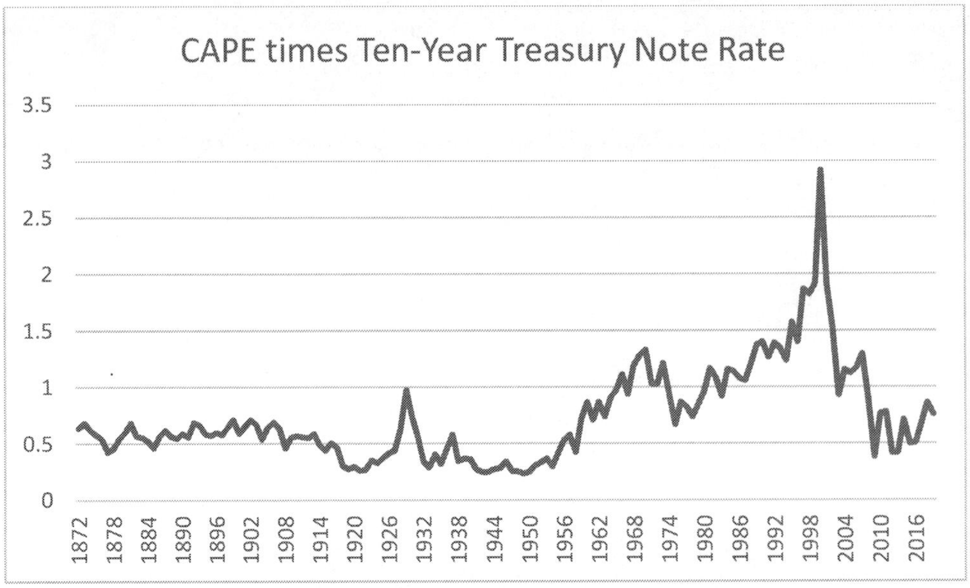

Using the Formula to incorporate the risk-free rate with CAPE (by multiplying the ten-year treasury note rate by the CAPE ratio), since 1872 the historic mean for the Formula is 0.73 with a standard deviation of 0.41 (indicating over-valuations at a ratio of 1.14 and under-valuation at a ratio of 0.32). Based on one standard deviation from the mean, the chart of the Formula since 1872, identifies historic expensiveness in 1929, 1967-1974, and 1983-2005. The chart of the Formula since 1872 identifies historic inexpensiveness in 1919-1924, 1933-1954, and 2009.

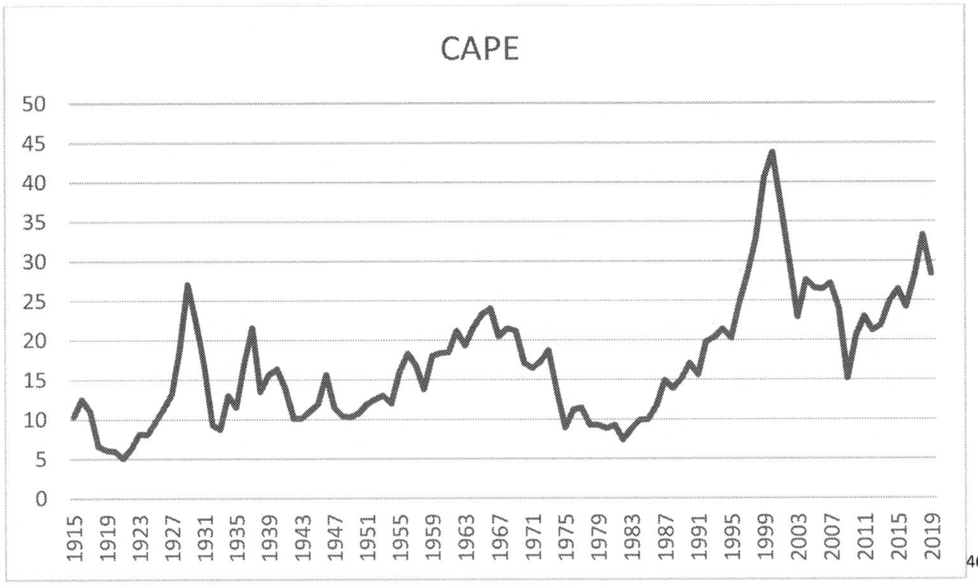

[46]

Focusing in on the last 100 years, the average CAPE ratio is 17.14 with a standard deviation of 6.75 (indicating over-valuation at a ratio value of 23.89 and under-valuation at a ratio value of 10.39). Based on one standard deviation from the mean, the chart of the CAPE ratio since 1915 identifies historic expensiveness in 1929, 1966, 1996-2008 and 2014-present. Based on one standard deviation from the

[46] https://www.multpl.com/shiller-pe

mean, the chart of the CAPE ratio since 1915 identifies historic inexpensiveness in 1918-1925, 1932-1933, 1942-1943, 1949, and 1975-1985.

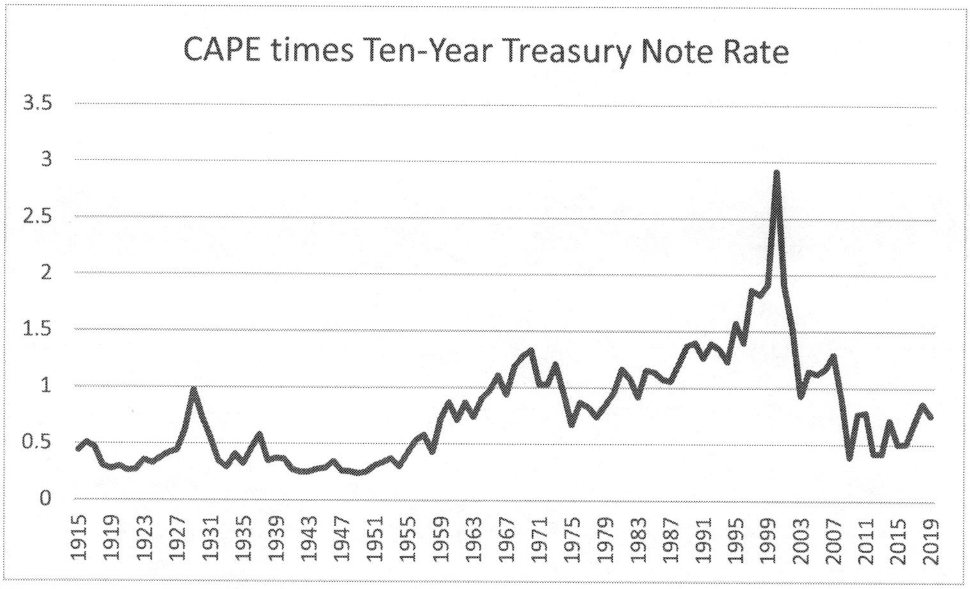

Using the Formula to consider the risk-free rate with CAPE over the last 100 years (by multiplying the ten-year treasury note rate by the CAPE ratio), since 1915 the historic mean for the Formula is 0.788 with a standard deviation of 0.478 (indicating over-valuation at a ratio of 1.266 and under-valuation at a ratio of 0.31). Based on one standard deviation from the mean, the chart of the Formula since 1915, identifies historic expensiveness in 1929, 1965-1974, and 1980-2009. The chart of the Formula since 1915 identifies historic inexpensiveness in 1919-1924, 1933-1954, and 2009.

From the analysis of 1872 to present and 1915 to present, it is clear that CAPE and the Formula are fairly consistent in identifying periods of relative expense historically. However, the primary difference between the two ratios is the magnitude by which relative expense is identified. By way of example, the highs identified in 1929 and 1970 are roughly identical on the CAPE ratio, whereas under the Formula analysis the 1970 high is higher than the expense in 1929. Similarly, CAPE identifies a historical overvaluation in 2018 which the Formula does not.

Part II (Apple PE Risk-Adjusted)

As a case study of the general applicability of the Formula consider the share price of Apple Inc. since January 1, 2017.

[47]

Beginning first with price it is clear that price has risen steadily since 2017 (with a decline between October 2018 and December 2018 after which the share price recovered back to previous highs). Looking just at the price one might conclude that the price was “expensive”. However, without looking at underlying value ratio this determination is highly speculative.

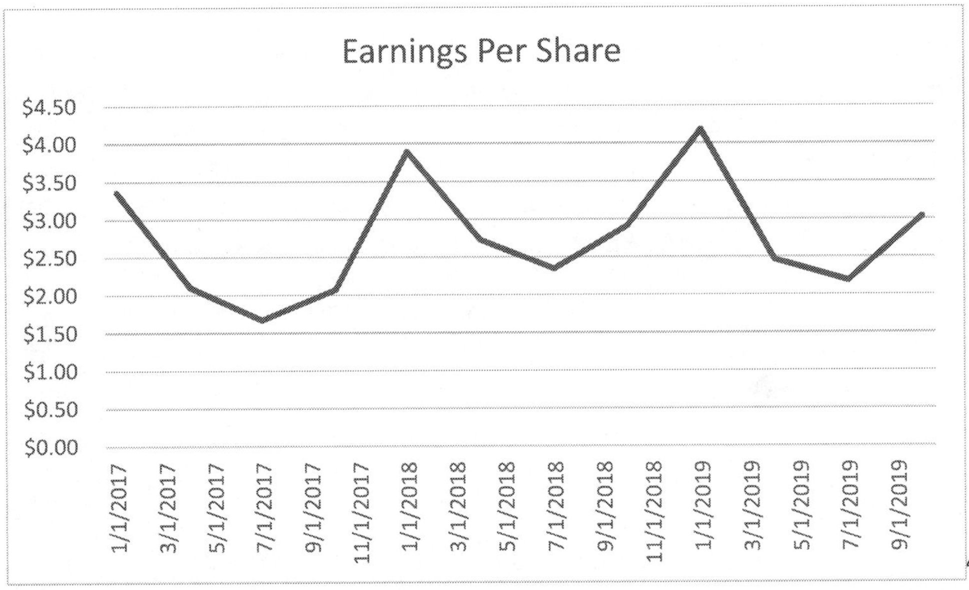

[48]

47 https://www.alphaquery.com/stock/AAPL/earnings-history
48 https://www.alphaquery.com/stock/AAPL/earnings-history

During the same period, earnings have oscillated within a range. From this oscillation one can intuit that given the relatively consistent price growth the share price of Apple Inc. was periodically over- and under-valued on a relative basis over this few year period.

[49]

The price to earnings ratio allows the viewer to measure the relative expense of the share price of Apple Inc. From the chart above, it is clear that the relative expense of Apple Inc's share price has varied within a consistent range over the last few years (in accordance with changes in earnings and share price). The mean for the time period was 66.17 with a standard deviation of 18.63 (indicating over-valuation at 84.80 and under-valuation at 47.54). Periods of under-valuation marked by approximately one standard deviation below the mean include before 3/1/2017, between 1/2/2018 through 4/2/2018 and 1/2/2019 through 4/2/2019. Periods of over-valuation marked by approximately one standard deviation above the mean include 7/1/2017, 7/1/2018-10/1/2018 and 3/1/2019 to the present.

[49] https://www.alphaquery.com/stock/AAPL/earnings-history

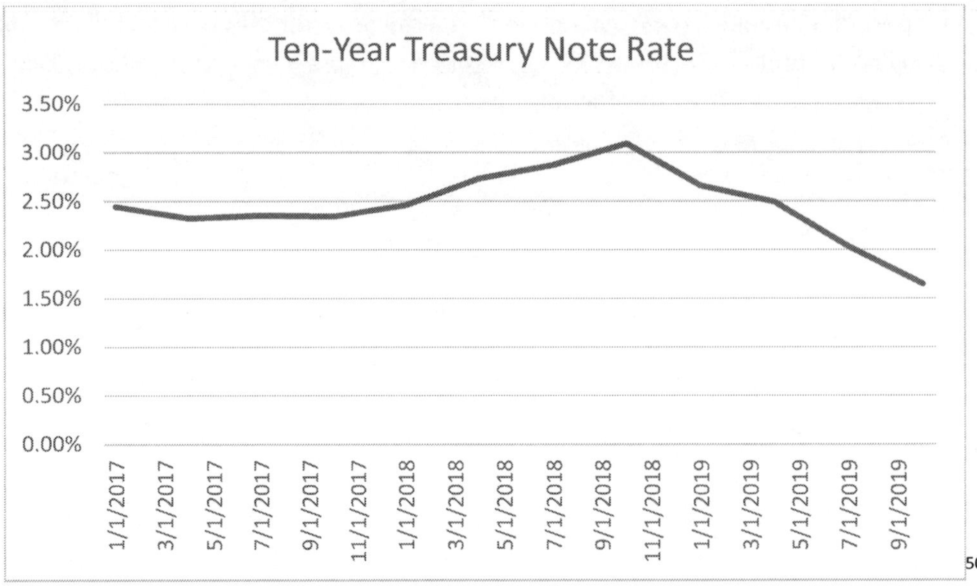

[50]

However, the price to earnings ratio alone does not account for movements in the risk-free rate. During the same period, the risk-free rate steadily rose until 10/1/2018 at which point the risk-free rate began to decline steadily (one might recall from recent history that the Federal Reserve board made the decision around the same time in 2018 to reverse a rate hiking cycle in favor of additional rate cuts).

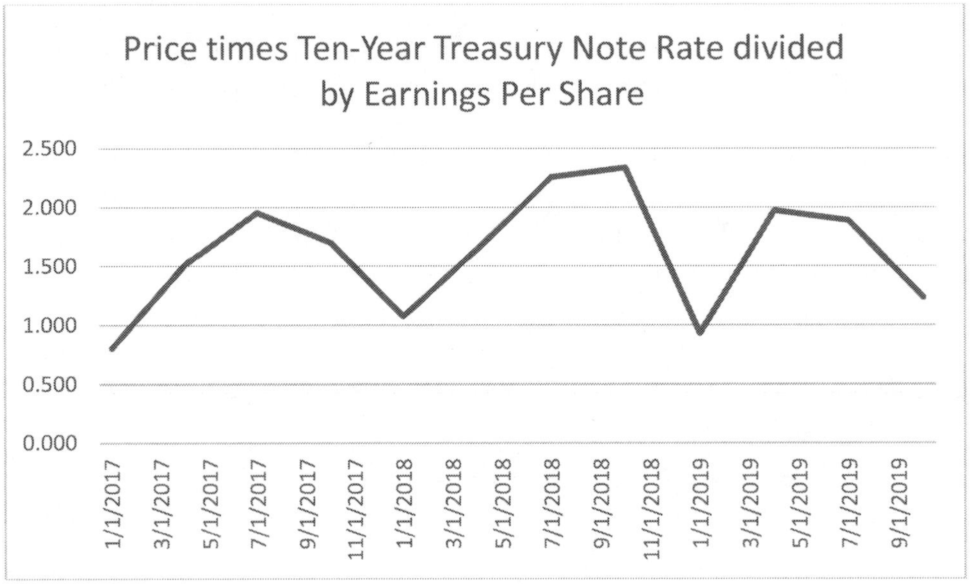

Adjusting for the risk-free rate provides a clearer picture of the relative expensiveness of the share price of Apple Inc. The mean for the time period was 1.61 with a standard deviation of 0.49 (indicating over-valuation at 2.09 and under-valuation at 1.12).

---

[50] Board of Governors of the Federal Reserve System (US), 10-Year Treasury Constant Maturity Rate [DGS10], retrieved from FRED, Federal Reserve Bank of St. Louis; https://fred.stlouisfed.org/series/DGS10, November 21, 2019.

Periods of under-valuation marked by approximately one standard deviation below the mean include 1/1/2017 to 3/1/2017, 1/2/2018 and 1/2/2019. Periods of over-valuation marked by approximately one standard deviation above the mean include 7/1/2017, 7/1/2018 to 10/1/2018 and 4/1/2019 to 7/1/2019. As of 9/1/2019, the Formula indicates relative under-valuation. These determinations of relative expense coincide with the P/E ratio with the exception of the period following 9/1/2019 (which as noted above marks a period of a decreasing risk-free rate). It is also notable that since 9/1/2019 until today (November 21, 2019) Apple Inc. shares have increased ~20% (a gain which one would expect from the Formula, but not from Price to Earnings considered alone).

Appendix B

Part A (Wilshire 5000 Datasets)

Observed Date Wilshire 5000 and GDP	Wilshire 5000 to GDP	Treasury Observation Date	Ten Year Treasury Note Rate	Wilshire 5000 times Ten Year Treasury note Rate divided by GDP
1971-01-01	0.25374	1/4/1971	6.46%	0.016391293
1971-04-01	0.26217	4/1/1971	5.58%	0.014629212
1971-07-01	0.25212	7/1/1971	6.69%	0.016867011
1971-10-01	0.24945	10/1/1971	6.00%	0.014966956
1972-01-01	0.26873	1/3/1972	5.94%	0.015962522
1972-04-01	0.26956	4/3/1972	6.14%	0.016551273
1972-07-01	0.26727	7/3/1972	6.14%	0.01641013
1972-10-01	0.27227	10/2/1972	6.54%	0.017806201
1973-01-01	0.25298	1/2/1973	6.43%	0.016266735
1973-04-01	0.22572	4/2/1973	6.74%	0.015213571
1973-07-01	0.23126	7/2/1973	7.01%	0.01621131
1973-10-01	0.21257	10/1/1973	6.91%	0.014688347
1974-01-01	0.20209	1/2/1974	6.94%	0.014025318
1974-04-01	0.17779	4/1/1974	7.42%	0.013191969
1974-07-01	0.14246	7/1/1974	7.65%	0.010898406
1974-10-01	0.13949	10/1/1974	7.97%	0.011117087
1975-01-01	0.16117	1/2/1975	7.42%	0.011958857
1975-04-01	0.18083	4/1/1975	8.08%	0.01461068
1975-07-01	0.16794	7/1/1975	7.97%	0.013384526
1975-10-01	0.16903	10/1/1975	8.47%	0.014317129
1976-01-01	0.18703	1/2/1976	7.77%	0.014531932
1976-04-01	0.18717	4/1/1976	7.68%	0.0143747
1976-07-01	0.18896	7/1/1976	7.88%	0.014889943
1976-10-01	0.18797	10/1/1976	7.49%	0.01407926
1977-01-01	0.18149	1/3/1977	6.84%	0.012414122
1977-04-01	0.17642	4/1/1977	7.43%	0.013108007
1977-07-01	0.17205	7/1/1977	7.34%	0.012628407
1977-10-01	0.16677	10/3/1977	7.41%	0.012357322
1978-01-01	0.15901	1/3/1978	7.83%	0.012450385
1978-04-01	0.16776	4/3/1978	8.13%	0.013638741
1978-07-01	0.17742	7/3/1978	8.59%	0.015240456
1978-10-01	0.15899	10/2/1978	8.58%	0.01364162
1979-01-01	0.16818	1/2/1979	9.18%	0.015439189
1979-04-01	0.17291	4/2/1979	9.11%	0.015751861
1979-07-01	0.18262	7/2/1979	8.76%	0.015997865
1979-10-01	0.18403	10/1/1979	9.51%	0.017500802
1980-01-01	0.18747	1/2/1980	10.50%	0.019684706
1980-04-01	0.18406	4/1/1980	12.69%	0.023357601

1980-07-01	0.21039	7/1/1980	10.13%	0.021312614
1980-10-01	0.22206	10/1/1980	11.78%	0.02615843
1981-01-01	0.21092	1/2/1981	12.42%	0.026195959
1981-04-01	0.21702	4/1/1981	13.14%	0.028516534
1981-07-01	0.20190	7/1/1981	14.04%	0.028346766
1981-10-01	0.19664	10/1/1981	15.75%	0.030971241
1982-01-01	0.18386	1/4/1982	14.19%	0.026089047
1982-04-01	0.18195	4/1/1982	14.10%	0.025654499
1982-07-01	0.18100	7/1/1982	14.40%	0.02606432
1982-10-01	0.21944	10/1/1982	11.51%	0.025257612
1983-01-01	0.23735	1/3/1983	10.32%	0.024494789
1983-04-01	0.25994	4/4/1983	10.60%	0.027553952
1983-07-01	0.25974	7/1/1983	10.93%	0.028389462
1983-10-01	0.25191	10/3/1983	11.47%	0.028893545
1984-01-01	0.23610	1/3/1984	11.86%	0.028001004
1984-04-01	0.22363	4/2/1984	12.56%	0.028088467
1984-07-01	0.22818	7/2/1984	13.87%	0.031648646
1984-10-01	0.23321	10/1/1984	12.54%	0.029244256
1985-01-01	0.24992	1/2/1985	11.70%	0.029240102
1985-04-01	0.25990	4/1/1985	11.66%	0.030303764
1985-07-01	0.26338	7/1/1985	10.19%	0.026838161
1985-10-01	0.27213	10/1/1985	10.29%	0.028002243
1986-01-01	0.30348	1/2/1986	9.04%	0.027434536
1986-04-01	0.33276	4/1/1986	7.37%	0.024524103
1986-07-01	0.32836	7/1/1986	7.37%	0.024200345
1986-10-01	0.32684	10/1/1986	7.41%	0.024219212
1987-01-01	0.37120	1/2/1987	7.18%	0.026652198
1987-04-01	0.38138	4/1/1987	7.59%	0.028947028
1987-07-01	0.40686	7/1/1987	8.36%	0.034013458
1987-10-01	0.31816	10/1/1987	9.66%	0.030733981
1988-01-01	0.32350	1/4/1988	8.83%	0.028564878
1988-04-01	0.32832	4/4/1988	8.68%	0.028498394
1988-07-01	0.33055	7/1/1988	8.77%	0.028988892
1988-10-01	0.33282	10/3/1988	8.84%	0.029421062
1989-01-01	0.34848	1/3/1989	9.23%	0.032164342
1989-04-01	0.37252	4/3/1989	9.21%	0.034309109
1989-07-01	0.40135	7/3/1989	8.09%	0.032469611
1989-10-01	0.40239	10/2/1989	8.28%	0.033317695
1990-01-01	0.38327	1/2/1990	7.94%	0.030431967
1990-04-01	0.39203	4/2/1990	8.65%	0.033910361
1990-07-01	0.37309	7/2/1990	8.43%	0.031451886
1990-10-01	0.35018	10/1/1990	8.71%	0.030500958
1991-01-01	0.39580	1/2/1991	7.97%	0.031545564
1991-04-01	0.42658	4/1/1991	8.07%	0.034425059
1991-07-01	0.43282	7/1/1991	8.26%	0.035750549
1991-10-01	0.43833	10/1/1991	7.45%	0.032655228

1992-01-01	0.46882	1/2/1992	6.78%	0.031785677
1992-04-01	0.45511	4/1/1992	7.46%	0.033951517
1992-07-01	0.45681	7/1/1992	7.10%	0.032433236
1992-10-01	0.46438	10/1/1992	6.23%	0.028930976
1993-01-01	0.48970	1/4/1993	6.60%	0.032319954
1993-04-01	0.48953	4/1/1993	6.06%	0.029665772
1993-07-01	0.50161	7/1/1993	5.80%	0.029093157
1993-10-01	0.50803	10/1/1993	5.34%	0.027128864
1994-01-01	0.51076	1/3/1994	5.92%	0.030236751
1994-04-01	0.48228	4/4/1994	7.16%	0.034530989
1994-07-01	0.48860	7/1/1994	7.34%	0.035863106
1994-10-01	0.48168	10/3/1994	7.66%	0.036897031
1995-01-01	0.50007	1/3/1995	7.88%	0.03940579
1995-04-01	0.54146	4/3/1995	7.14%	0.038660189
1995-07-01	0.58600	7/3/1995	6.21%	0.036390519
1995-10-01	0.61137	10/2/1995	6.15%	0.037599326
1996-01-01	0.64353	1/2/1996	5.60%	0.036037617
1996-04-01	0.66501	4/1/1996	6.31%	0.041962154
1996-07-01	0.65307	7/1/1996	6.74%	0.044016902
1996-10-01	0.70328	10/1/1996	6.65%	0.046768078
1997-01-01	0.74603	1/2/1997	6.54%	0.048790104
1997-04-01	0.76093	4/1/1997	6.90%	0.05250431
1997-07-01	0.85636	7/1/1997	6.45%	0.05523532
1997-10-01	0.87569	10/1/1997	6.04%	0.052891855
1998-01-01	0.92597	1/2/1998	5.67%	0.052502296
1998-04-01	0.98957	4/1/1998	5.62%	0.055613708
1998-07-01	0.93360	7/1/1998	5.44%	0.050788074
1998-10-01	0.93616	10/1/1998	4.33%	0.040535621
1999-01-01	1.04371	1/4/1999	4.69%	0.048949799
1999-04-01	1.09359	4/1/1999	5.27%	0.057632322
1999-07-01	1.08621	7/1/1999	5.85%	0.06354332
1999-10-01	1.10386	10/1/1999	6.00%	0.066231897
2000-01-01	1.18256	1/3/2000	6.58%	0.077812149
2000-04-01	1.13624	4/3/2000	6.00%	0.068174603
2000-07-01	1.16416	7/3/2000	6.00%	0.069849593
2000-10-01	1.05537	10/2/2000	5.83%	0.061528123
2001-01-01	0.97752	1/2/2001	4.92%	0.048094118
2001-04-01	0.94024	4/2/2001	4.98%	0.046823923
2001-07-01	0.88461	7/2/2001	5.37%	0.047503461
2001-10-01	0.85128	10/1/2001	4.55%	0.038733381
2002-01-01	0.86691	1/2/2002	5.20%	0.045079296
2002-04-01	0.82464	4/1/2002	5.44%	0.044860346
2002-07-01	0.68662	7/1/2002	4.85%	0.033300853
2002-10-01	0.67638	10/1/2002	3.72%	0.025161197
2003-01-01	0.65486	1/2/2003	4.07%	0.026652809
2003-04-01	0.71238	4/1/2003	3.84%	0.027355539

2003-07-01	0.75636	7/1/2003	3.56%	0.026926283
2003-10-01	0.79477	10/1/2003	3.96%	0.031473052
2004-01-01	0.84678	1/2/2004	4.38%	0.037089132
2004-04-01	0.82902	4/1/2004	3.91%	0.032414489
2004-07-01	0.80308	7/1/2004	4.57%	0.036700702
2004-10-01	0.84261	10/1/2004	4.21%	0.035474077
2005-01-01	0.85387	1/3/2005	4.23%	0.03611863
2005-04-01	0.84265	4/1/2005	4.46%	0.037581985
2005-07-01	0.87099	7/1/2005	4.06%	0.035362148
2005-10-01	0.86786	10/3/2005	4.39%	0.038099042
2006-01-01	0.89808	1/3/2006	4.37%	0.039245962
2006-04-01	0.89279	4/3/2006	4.88%	0.043568225
2006-07-01	0.88553	7/3/2006	5.15%	0.045604674
2006-10-01	0.94997	10/2/2006	4.62%	0.04388877
2007-01-01	0.97332	1/2/2007	4.68%	0.04555136
2007-04-01	1.01395	4/2/2007	4.65%	0.047148667
2007-07-01	0.99959	7/2/2007	5.00%	0.04997942
2007-10-01	1.00000	10/1/2007	4.56%	0.0456
2008-01-01	0.90781	1/2/2008	3.91%	0.035495532
2008-04-01	0.92217	4/1/2008	3.57%	0.032921622
2008-07-01	0.84951	7/1/2008	4.01%	0.034065305
2008-10-01	0.62352	10/1/2008	3.77%	0.023506842
2009-01-01	0.56744	1/2/2009	2.46%	0.013958961
2009-04-01	0.63990	4/1/2009	2.68%	0.0171494
2009-07-01	0.71803	7/1/2009	3.55%	0.025489981
2009-10-01	0.77680	10/1/2009	3.21%	0.024935259
2010-01-01	0.80780	1/4/2010	3.85%	0.031100122
2010-04-01	0.81449	4/1/2010	3.89%	0.031683609
2010-07-01	0.78205	7/1/2010	2.96%	0.023148757
2010-10-01	0.86223	10/1/2010	2.54%	0.021900542
2011-01-01	0.93597	1/3/2011	3.36%	0.031448638
2011-04-01	0.93899	4/1/2011	3.46%	0.03248908
2011-07-01	0.86708	7/1/2011	3.22%	0.027919979
2011-10-01	0.85552	10/3/2011	1.80%	0.015399359
2012-01-01	0.93642	1/3/2012	1.97%	0.018447434
2012-04-01	0.92926	4/2/2012	2.22%	0.020629476
2012-07-01	0.95997	7/2/2012	1.61%	0.015455476
2012-10-01	0.97266	10/1/2012	1.64%	0.015951705
2013-01-01	1.04016	1/2/2013	1.86%	0.019347055
2013-04-01	1.10553	4/1/2013	1.86%	0.020562891
2013-07-01	1.14976	7/1/2013	2.50%	0.028744072
2013-10-01	1.20625	10/1/2013	2.66%	0.032086168
2014-01-01	1.26226	1/2/2014	3.00%	0.037867737
2014-04-01	1.27759	4/1/2014	2.77%	0.035389321
2014-07-01	1.30921	7/1/2014	2.58%	0.033777682
2014-10-01	1.31968	10/1/2014	2.42%	0.031936295

2015-01-01	1.35700	1/2/2015	2.12%	0.028768372
2015-04-01	1.37403	4/1/2015	1.87%	0.025694361
2015-07-01	1.31757	7/1/2015	2.43%	0.032016876
2015-10-01	1.32416	10/1/2015	2.05%	0.027145249
2016-01-01	1.24556	1/4/2016	2.24%	0.027900629
2016-04-01	1.32417	4/1/2016	1.79%	0.02370257
2016-07-01	1.38096	7/1/2016	1.46%	0.020161954
2016-10-01	1.39560	10/3/2016	1.62%	0.022638017
2017-01-01	1.47953	1/2/2017	2.44%	0.036164177
2017-04-01	1.51540	4/3/2017	2.32%	0.035146782
2017-07-01	1.54324	7/3/2017	2.35%	0.03626455
2017-10-01	1.61133	10/2/2017	2.34%	0.037718061
2018-01-01	1.67748	1/2/2018	2.46%	0.041265911
2018-04-01	1.64762	4/2/2018	2.73%	0.044980162
2018-07-01	1.72651	7/2/2018	2.87%	0.049550784
2018-10-01	1.61365	10/1/2018	3.09%	0.049861741
2019-01-01	1.62668	1/2/2019	2.66%	0.043269602
2019-04-01	1.70595	4/1/2019	2.49%	0.042478191
2019-07-01	1.73349	7/1/2019	2.03%	0.035189751
			Average	**0.030827331**
			Standard Deviation	**0.012679309**

Part B (S&P Datasets)

Date	Ten Year Treasury Note Rate	Nominal GDP (100 millions of Dollars)	The S&P Index Average for January	S&P to GDP	Product of Price times Ten Year Treasury Note Rate	S&P times Ten-Year Treasury Note Rate divided by GDP
1871	5.32%	76.650	4.44	0.0579	0.236208	0.0030816
1872	5.36%	83.090	4.86	0.0585	0.260496	0.0031351
1873	5.58%	88.370	5.11	0.0578	0.285138	0.0032266
1874	5.47%	85.630	4.66	0.0544	0.254902	0.0029768
1875	5.07%	82.390	4.55	0.0552	0.230685	0.0027999
1876	4.59%	83.880	4.46	0.0532	0.204714	0.0024406
1877	4.45%	86.040	3.55	0.0413	0.157975	0.0018361
1878	4.34%	84.600	3.24	0.0383	0.140616	0.0016621
1879	4.22%	94.490	3.58	0.0379	0.151076	0.0015989
1880	4.02%	104.620	5.11	0.0488	0.205422	0.0019635
1881	3.70%	117.400	6.19	0.0527	0.22903	0.0019509
1882	3.62%	123.310	5.91	0.0479	0.213942	0.0017350
1883	3.63%	124.350	5.82	0.0468	0.211266	0.0016990
1884	3.62%	118.960	5.18	0.0435	0.187516	0.0015763
1885	3.52%	117.050	4.24	0.0362	0.149248	0.0012751
1886	3.37%	122.970	5.21	0.0424	0.175577	0.0014278
1887	3.52%	132.730	5.58	0.0420	0.196416	0.0014798
1888	3.67%	140.000	5.31	0.0379	0.194877	0.0013920
1889	3.45%	139.870	5.23	0.0374	0.180435	0.0012900
1890	3.42%	152.230	5.38	0.0353	0.183996	0.0012087
1891	3.62%	155.580	4.83	0.0310	0.174846	0.0011238
1892	3.60%	165.140	5.5	0.0333	0.198	0.0011990
1893	3.75%	155.660	5.62	0.0361	0.21075	0.0013539
1894	3.70%	142.800	4.32	0.0303	0.15984	0.0011193
1895	3.46%	157.540	4.25	0.0270	0.14705	0.0009334
1896	3.60%	156.430	4.27	0.0273	0.15372	0.0009827
1897	3.40%	163.090	4.22	0.0259	0.14348	0.0008798
1898	3.35%	182.630	4.88	0.0267	0.16348	0.0008951
1899	3.10%	196.940	6.09	0.0309	0.18879	0.0009586
1900	3.15%	207.660	6.1	0.0294	0.19215	0.0009253
1901	3.10%	224.840	7.07	0.0314	0.21917	0.0009748
1902	3.18%	242.940	8.11	0.0334	0.257898	0.0010616
1903	3.30%	261.800	8.46	0.0323	0.27918	0.0010664
1904	3.40%	259.280	6.69	0.0258	0.22746	0.0008773
1905	3.48%	290.660	8.44	0.0290	0.293712	0.0010105
1906	3.43%	313.360	9.88	0.0315	0.338884	0.0010815
1907	3.67%	341.780	9.56	0.0280	0.350852	0.0010265

1908	3.87%	304.230	6.85	0.0225	0.265095	0.0008714
1909	3.76%	325.400	9.06	0.0278	0.340656	0.0010469
1910	3.91%	337.460	10.09	0.0299	0.394519	0.0011691
1911	3.98%	346.750	9.27	0.0267	0.368946	0.0010640
1912	4.01%	377.450	9.12	0.0242	0.365712	0.0009689
1913	4.45%	395.170	9.29	0.0235	0.413405	0.0010461
1914	4.16%	368.310	8.36	0.0227	0.347776	0.0009442
1915	4.24%	390.480	7.48	0.0192	0.317152	0.0008122
1916	4.05%	501.170	9.34	0.0186	0.37827	0.0007548
1917	4.23%	602.780	9.57	0.0159	0.404811	0.0006716
1918	4.57%	765.670	7.22	0.0094	0.329954	0.0004309
1919	4.50%	790.900	7.85	0.0099	0.35325	0.0004466
1920	4.97%	892.460	8.82	0.0099	0.438354	0.0004912
1921	5.09%	743.140	7.11	0.0096	0.361899	0.0004870
1922	4.30%	741.400	7.29	0.0098	0.31347	0.0004228
1923	4.36%	862.380	8.9	0.0103	0.38804	0.0004500
1924	4.06%	877.860	8.84	0.0101	0.358904	0.0004088
1925	3.86%	914.490	10.57	0.0116	0.408002	0.0004462
1926	3.68%	978.850	12.65	0.0129	0.46552	0.0004756
1927	3.34%	964.660	13.4	0.0139	0.44756	0.0004640
1928	3.33%	983.050	17.53	0.0178	0.583749	0.0005938
1929	3.60%	1,046.000	24.86	0.0238	0.89496	0.0008556
1930	3.29%	922.000	21.71	0.0235	0.714259	0.0007747
1931	3.34%	774.000	15.98	0.0206	0.533732	0.0006896
1932	3.68%	595.000	8.3	0.0139	0.30544	0.0005133
1933	3.31%	572.000	7.09	0.0124	0.234679	0.0004103
1934	3.12%	668.000	10.54	0.0158	0.328848	0.0004923
1935	2.79%	742.000	9.26	0.0125	0.258354	0.0003482
1936	2.65%	848.000	13.76	0.0162	0.36464	0.0004300
1937	2.68%	930.000	17.59	0.0189	0.471412	0.0005069
1938	2.56%	874.000	11.31	0.0129	0.289536	0.0003313
1939	2.36%	934.000	12.5	0.0134	0.295	0.0003158
1940	2.21%	1,029.000	12.3	0.0120	0.27183	0.0002642
1941	1.95%	1,293.000	10.55	0.0082	0.205725	0.0001591
1942	2.46%	1,660.000	8.93	0.0054	0.219678	0.0001323
1943	2.47%	2,031.000	10.09	0.0050	0.249223	0.0001227
1944	2.48%	2,244.000	11.85	0.0053	0.29388	0.0001310
1945	2.37%	2,280.000	13.49	0.0059	0.319713	0.0001402
1946	2.19%	2,275.000	18.02	0.0079	0.394638	0.0001735
1947	2.25%	2,496.000	15.21	0.0061	0.342225	0.0001371
1948	2.44%	2,745.000	14.83	0.0054	0.361852	0.0001318
1949	2.31%	2,725.000	15.36	0.0056	0.354816	0.0001302
1950	2.32%	2,998.000	16.88	0.0056	0.391616	0.0001306

1951	2.57%	3,469.000	21.21	0.0061	0.545097	0.0001571
1952	2.68%	3,673.000	24.19	0.0066	0.648292	0.0001765
1953	2.83%	3,892.000	26.18	0.0067	0.740894	0.0001904
1954	2.48%	3,905.000	25.46	0.0065	0.631408	0.0001617
1955	2.61%	4,255.000	35.6	0.0084	0.92916	0.0002184
1956	2.90%	4,494.000	44.15	0.0098	1.28035	0.0002849
1957	3.46%	4,740.000	45.43	0.0096	1.571878	0.0003316
1958	3.09%	4,812.000	41.12	0.0085	1.270608	0.0002640
1959	4.02%	5,217.000	55.62	0.0107	2.235924	0.0004286
1960	4.72%	5,424.000	58.03	0.0107	2.739016	0.0005050
1961	3.84%	5,622.000	59.72	0.0106	2.293248	0.0004079
1962	4.08%	6,039.000	69.07	0.0114	2.818056	0.0004666
1963	3.83%	6,375.000	65.06	0.0102	2.491798	0.0003909
1964	4.17%	6,845.000	76.45	0.0112	3.187965	0.0004657
1965	4.19%	7,423.000	86.12	0.0116	3.608428	0.0004861
1966	4.61%	8,134.000	93.32	0.0115	4.302052	0.0005289
1967	4.58%	8,600.000	84.45	0.0098	3.86781	0.0004497
1968	5.53%	9,407.000	95.04	0.0101	5.255712	0.0005587
1969	6.04%	10,176.000	102.04	0.0100	6.163216	0.0006057
1970	7.79%	10,733.000	90.33	0.0084	7.036707	0.0006556
1971	6.24%	11,649.000	93.49	0.0080	5.833776	0.0005008
1972	5.95%	12,791.000	103.3	0.0081	6.14635	0.0004805
1973	6.46%	14,254.000	118.42	0.0083	7.649932	0.0005367
1974	6.99%	15,452.000	96.11	0.0062	6.718089	0.0004348
1975	7.50%	16,849.000	72.56	0.0043	5.442	0.0003230
1976	7.74%	18,734.000	96.86	0.0052	7.496964	0.0004002
1977	7.21%	20,818.000	103.81	0.0050	7.484701	0.0003595
1978	7.96%	23,516.000	90.25	0.0038	7.1839	0.0003055
1979	9.10%	26,273.000	99.71	0.0038	9.07361	0.0003454
1980	10.80%	28,573.000	110.87	0.0039	11.97396	0.0004191
1981	12.57%	32,070.000	132.97	0.0041	16.714329	0.0005212
1982	14.59%	33,438.000	117.28	0.0035	17.111152	0.0005117
1983	10.46%	36,340.000	144.27	0.0040	15.090642	0.0004153
1984	11.67%	40,376.000	166.39	0.0041	19.417713	0.0004809
1985	11.38%	43,390.000	171.61	0.0040	19.529218	0.0004501
1986	9.19%	45,796.000	208.19	0.0045	19.132661	0.0004178
1987	7.08%	48,552.000	264.51	0.0054	18.727308	0.0003857
1988	8.67%	52,364.000	250.48	0.0048	21.716616	0.0004147
1989	9.09%	56,416.000	285.41	0.0051	25.943769	0.0004599
1990	8.21%	59,631.000	339.97	0.0057	27.911537	0.0004681
1991	8.09%	61,581.000	325.5	0.0053	26.33295	0.0004276
1992	7.03%	65,203.000	416.08	0.0064	29.250424	0.0004486
1993	6.60%	68,586.000	435.23	0.0063	28.72518	0.0004188

1994	5.75%	72,872.000	472.99	0.0065	27.196925	0.0003732
1995	7.78%	76,397.000	465.25	0.0061	36.19645	0.0004738
1996	5.65%	80,731.000	614.42	0.0076	34.71473	0.0004300
1997	6.58%	85,776.000	766.22	0.0089	50.417276	0.0005878
1998	5.54%	90,628.000	963.36	0.0106	53.370144	0.0005889
1999	4.72%	96,307.000	1,248.77	0.0130	58.941944	0.0006120
2000	6.66%	102,523.000	1,425.59	0.0139	94.944294	0.0009261
2001	5.16%	105,818.000	1,335.64	0.0126	68.919024	0.0006513
2002	5.04%	109,364.000	1,140.21	0.0104	57.466584	0.0005255
2003	4.05%	114,582.000	895.84	0.0078	36.28152	0.0003166
2004	4.15%	122,137.000	1,132.52	0.0093	46.99958	0.0003848
2005	4.22%	130,366.000	1,181.41	0.0091	49.855502	0.0003824
2006	4.42%	138,146.000	1,278.73	0.0093	56.519866	0.0004091
2007	4.76%	144,519.000	1,424.16	0.0099	67.790016	0.0004691
2008	3.74%	147,128.000	1,378.76	0.0094	51.565624	0.0003505
2009	2.52%	144,489.000	865.58	0.0060	21.812616	0.0001510
2010	3.73%	149,921.000	1,123.58	0.0075	41.909534	0.0002795
2011	3.39%	155,426.000	1,282.62	0.0083	43.480818	0.0002798
2012	1.97%	161,970.000	1,300.58	0.0080	25.621426	0.0001582
2013	1.91%	167,849.000	1,480.40	0.0088	28.27564	0.0001685
2014	2.86%	175,273.000	1,822.36	0.0104	52.119496	0.0002974
2015	1.88%	182,248.000	2,028.18	0.0111	38.129784	0.0002092
2016	2.09%	187,150.000	1,918.59	0.0103	40.098531	0.0002143
2017	2.43%	195,194.000	2,275.12	0.0117	55.285416	0.0002832
2018	2.58%	205,802.000	2,791.73	0.0136	72.026634	0.0003500

	S&P to GDP	S&P times Ten Year Treasury Note Rate divided by GDP
Average	0.0095	0.0004058
Standard Deviation	0.0042	0.00016843
Two Standard Deviations	0.0084	0.000336861
Three Standard Deviations	0.0127	0.000505291

Pearson Coefficient	
Price & Value	0.964
Price & Risk-free Rate	-0.155409611
Price and Product of Price and 10 Year	0.881515644
Price and Price to Value	0.05053459
Price to Value and Formula	0.577354234
Risk-free and Formula	0.375881894

Part C (Housing Datasets)

Observed Date of Mortgage Rates	30 Year Mortgage Rate	15 Year Mortgage Rate	Observed Dates of Household Income per Capita (Reported as of January 1st)	Household income per Capital (in hundreds)
1/3/1992	8.24	7.79	1992	538.97
1/8/1993	8.07	7.60	1993	536.10
1/7/1994	7.23	6.74	1994	542.33
1/6/1995	9.22	8.87	1995	559.31
1/5/1996	7.02	6.56	1996	567.44
1/3/1997	7.67	7.18	1997	579.11
1/2/1998	7.03	6.61	1998	600.40
1/8/1999	6.79	6.43	1999	615.26
1/7/2000	8.15	7.73	2000	613.99
1/5/2001	7.07	6.74	2001	600.38
1/4/2002	7.14	6.62	2002	593.60
1/3/2003	5.85	5.24	2003	592.86
1/8/2004	5.87	5.17	2004	590.80
1/6/2005	5.77	5.21	2005	597.12
1/5/2006	6.21	5.76	2006	601.78
1/4/2007	6.18	5.94	2007	609.85
1/3/2008	6.07	5.68	2008	588.11
1/8/2009	5.01	4.62	2009	584.00
1/7/2010	5.09	4.50	2010	568.73
1/6/2011	4.77	4.13	2011	560.06
1/5/2012	3.91	3.23	2012	559.00
1/3/2013	3.34	2.64	2013	578.56
1/2/2014	4.53	3.55	2014	569.69
1/8/2015	3.73	3.05	2015	599.01
1/7/2016	3.97	3.26	2016	617.79
1/5/2017	4.20	3.44	2017	626.26
1/4/2018	3.95	3.38	2018	631.79

Observed Date of Nominal Housing Price	Nominal Housing Price	Price times 15 year mortgage	Price times 30 year mortgage	Price to Income	Price times 15 year mortgage divided by Income	Price times 30 year mortgage divided Income
1992	75.70	589.66405	623.7268	0.14	1.09	1.16
1993	76.40	580.6248	616.53186	0.14	1.08	1.15
1994	78.20	527.09496	565.41492	0.14	0.97	1.04

1995	80.04	709.91932	737.93192	0.14	1.27	1.32
1996	81.45	534.29888	571.76496	0.14	0.94	1.01
1997	83.55	599.91772	640.85918	0.14	1.04	1.11
1998	87.19	576.34573	612.96679	0.15	0.96	1.02
1999	92.74	596.3182	629.7046	0.15	0.97	1.02
2000	100.00	773	815	0.16	1.26	1.33
2001	109.22	736.1091	772.15005	0.18	1.23	1.29
2002	116.44	770.81956	831.36732	0.20	1.30	1.40
2003	127.65	668.89648	746.7642	0.22	1.13	1.26
2004	140.71	727.47587	825.97357	0.24	1.23	1.40
2005	160.14	834.30856	923.98472	0.27	1.40	1.55
2006	180.83	1041.59808	1122.97293	0.30	1.73	1.87
2007	182.72	1085.37462	1129.22814	0.30	1.78	1.85
2008	171.08	971.75712	1038.47988	0.29	1.65	1.77
2009	149.37	690.09864	748.35372	0.26	1.18	1.28
2010	145.00	652.5135	738.06527	0.25	1.15	1.30
2011	139.05	574.27237	663.26373	0.25	1.03	1.18
2012	134.17	433.35618	524.58906	0.24	0.78	0.94
2013	144.32	380.99424	482.01544	0.25	0.66	0.83
2014	159.39	565.83805	722.04123	0.28	0.99	1.27
2015	166.30	507.20585	620.28781	0.28	0.85	1.04
2016	175.11	570.8423	695.16685	0.28	0.92	1.13
2017	184.80	635.6948	776.139	0.30	1.02	1.24
2018	196.35	663.6461	775.56275	0.31	1.05	1.23

Part D (Cyclical PE Datasets)

Date	CAPE	Ten Year Treasury Note Rate	CAPE times Ten Year Treasury Note Rate
1872	11.9	5.36%	0.63784
1873	12.25	5.58%	0.68355
1874	11.33	5.47%	0.619751
1875	11.41	5.07%	0.578487
1876	11.79	4.59%	0.541161
1877	9.52	4.45%	0.42364
1878	10.57	4.34%	0.458738
1879	12.87	4.22%	0.543114
1880	14.87	4.02%	0.597774
1881	18.47	3.70%	0.68339
1882	15.68	3.62%	0.567616
1883	15.27	3.63%	0.554301
1884	14.43	3.62%	0.522366
1885	13.13	3.52%	0.462176
1886	16.7	3.37%	0.56279
1887	17.52	3.52%	0.616704
1888	15.36	3.67%	0.563712
1889	15.81	3.45%	0.545445
1890	17.22	3.42%	0.588924
1891	15.43	3.62%	0.558566
1892	19.01	3.60%	0.68436
1893	17.65	3.75%	0.661875
1894	15.74	3.70%	0.58238
1895	16.51	3.46%	0.571246
1896	16.58	3.60%	0.59688
1897	17.03	3.40%	0.57902
1898	19.25	3.35%	0.644875
1899	22.92	3.10%	0.71052
1900	18.67	3.15%	0.588105
1901	20.97	3.10%	0.65007
1902	22.34	3.18%	0.710412
1903	20.32	3.30%	0.67056
1904	15.86	3.40%	0.53924
1905	18.46	3.48%	0.642408
1906	20.13	3.43%	0.690459
1907	17.22	3.67%	0.631974

1908	11.9	3.87%	0.46053
1909	14.77	3.76%	0.555352
1910	14.54	3.91%	0.568514
1911	14.05	3.98%	0.55919
1912	13.8	4.01%	0.55338
1913	13.15	4.45%	0.585175
1914	11.64	4.16%	0.484224
1915	10.36	4.24%	0.439264
1916	12.54	4.05%	0.50787
1917	10.99	4.23%	0.464877
1918	6.64	4.57%	0.303448
1919	6.1	4.50%	0.2745
1920	5.99	4.97%	0.297703
1921	5.12	5.09%	0.260608
1922	6.29	4.30%	0.27047
1923	8.15	4.36%	0.35534
1924	8.07	4.06%	0.327642
1925	9.69	3.86%	0.374034
1926	11.34	3.68%	0.417312
1927	13.19	3.34%	0.440546
1928	18.81	3.33%	0.626373
1929	27.08	3.60%	0.97488
1930	22.31	3.29%	0.733999
1931	16.71	3.34%	0.558114
1932	9.31	3.68%	0.342608
1933	8.73	3.31%	0.288963
1934	13.03	3.12%	0.406536
1935	11.5	2.79%	0.32085
1936	17.09	2.65%	0.452885
1937	21.62	2.68%	0.579416
1938	13.51	2.56%	0.345856
1939	15.6	2.36%	0.36816
1940	16.38	2.21%	0.361998
1941	13.9	1.95%	0.27105
1942	10.1	2.46%	0.24846
1943	10.15	2.47%	0.250705
1944	11.05	2.48%	0.27404
1945	11.96	2.37%	0.283452
1946	15.62	2.19%	0.342078
1947	11.47	2.25%	0.258075
1948	10.42	2.44%	0.254248
1949	10.25	2.31%	0.236775
1950	10.75	2.32%	0.2494

1951	11.9	2.57%	0.30583
1952	12.53	2.68%	0.335804
1953	13.01	2.83%	0.368183
1954	12	2.48%	0.2976
1955	15.99	2.61%	0.417339
1956	18.29	2.90%	0.53041
1957	16.72	3.46%	0.578512
1958	13.79	3.09%	0.426111
1959	17.98	4.02%	0.722796
1960	18.34	4.72%	0.865648
1961	18.47	3.84%	0.709248
1962	21.2	4.08%	0.86496
1963	19.26	3.83%	0.737658
1964	21.63	4.17%	0.901971
1965	23.27	4.19%	0.975013
1966	24.06	4.61%	1.109166
1967	20.43	4.58%	0.935694
1968	21.51	5.53%	1.189503
1969	21.19	6.04%	1.279876
1970	17.09	7.79%	1.331311
1971	16.46	6.24%	1.027104
1972	17.26	5.95%	1.02697
1973	18.71	6.46%	1.208666
1974	13.53	6.99%	0.945747
1975	8.92	7.50%	0.669
1976	11.19	7.74%	0.866106
1977	11.44	7.21%	0.824824
1978	9.24	7.96%	0.735504
1979	9.26	9.10%	0.84266
1980	8.85	10.80%	0.9558
1981	9.26	12.57%	1.163982
1982	7.39	14.59%	1.078201
1983	8.76	10.46%	0.916296
1984	9.89	11.67%	1.154163
1985	10	11.38%	1.138
1986	11.72	9.19%	1.077068
1987	14.92	7.08%	1.056336
1988	13.9	8.67%	1.20513
1989	15.09	9.09%	1.371681
1990	17.05	8.21%	1.399805
1991	15.61	8.09%	1.262849
1992	19.77	7.03%	1.389831
1993	20.32	6.60%	1.34112

1994	21.41	5.75%	1.231075
1995	20.22	7.78%	1.573116
1996	24.76	5.65%	1.39894
1997	28.33	6.58%	1.864114
1998	32.86	5.54%	1.820444
1999	40.57	4.72%	1.914904
2000	43.77	6.66%	2.915082
2001	36.98	5.16%	1.908168
2002	30.28	5.04%	1.526112
2003	22.9	4.05%	0.92745
2004	27.66	4.15%	1.14789
2005	26.59	4.22%	1.122098
2006	26.47	4.42%	1.169974
2007	27.21	4.76%	1.295196
2008	24.02	3.74%	0.898348
2009	15.17	2.52%	0.382284
2010	20.53	3.73%	0.765769
2011	22.98	3.39%	0.779022
2012	21.21	1.97%	0.417837
2013	21.9	1.91%	0.41829
2014	24.86	2.86%	0.710996
2015	26.49	1.88%	0.498012
2016	24.21	2.09%	0.505989
2017	28.06	2.43%	0.681858
2018	33.31	2.58%	0.859398
2019	28.38	2.66%	0.754908

	Cyclical Price to Earnings	Cyclical Price to Earnings times Ten-Year Treasury Note Rate
Average since 1872	16.7175	0.729865
Standard Deviation	6.75348	0.414815
Average since 1915	17.1443	0.788469
Standard Deviation	7.71449	0.478309

Part E (Apple Stock PE Dataset)

Observed Date of Price and EPS	Price	Earnings Per Share (EPS)	Price to Earnings Ratio	Observed Date of Ten-year treasury note rate	Ten-year treasury note rate	Price to Earnings times Ten-year treasury note rate
12/31/2016	$110.63	$3.36	32.93	1/2/2017	2.44%	0.804
3/31/2017	$137.50	$2.10	65.48	4/3/2017	2.32%	1.519
6/30/2017	$138.87	$1.67	83.16	7/3/2017	2.35%	1.954
9/30/2017	$150.19	$2.07	72.56	10/2/2017	2.34%	1.698
12/31/2017	$169.85	$3.89	43.66	1/2/2018	2.46%	1.074
3/31/2018	$164.09	$2.73	60.11	4/2/2018	2.73%	1.641
6/30/2018	$183.89	$2.34	78.59	7/2/2018	2.87%	2.255
9/30/2018	$220.19	$2.91	75.67	10/1/2018	3.09%	2.338
12/31/2018	$146.06	$4.18	34.94	1/2/2019	2.66%	0.929
3/31/2019	$194.91	$2.46	79.23	4/1/2019	2.49%	1.973
6/30/2019	$202.85	$2.18	93.05	7/1/2019	2.03%	1.889
9/30/2019	$226.34	$3.03	74.70	10/1/2019	1.65%	1.233

	Price to Earnings Ratio	Price to Earnings times Ten-Year Treasury Note Rate
Average	66.17	1.61
Standard Deviation	18.63	0.49

Made in the USA
Monee, IL
04 November 2026

67385527R10044